PROPHETS, POLITICS & NATIONS

EMMA STARK

PROPHETS, POLITICS & NATIONS

UNDERSTANDING THE
VITAL ROLE THAT PROPHETIC
VOICES PLAY IN SHAPING HISTORY

DESTINY IMAGE® PUBLISHERS, INC.

P.O. Box 310, Shippensburg, PA 17257-0310

"Publishing cutting-edge prophetic resources to supernaturally empower the body of Christ"

This book and all other Destiny Image and Destiny Image Fiction books are available at Christian bookstores and distributors worldwide.

For more information on foreign distributors, call 717-532-3040.

Reach us on the Internet: www.destinyimage.com.

ISBN 13 TP: 978-0-7684-7756-6

ISBN 13 eBook: 978-0-7684-7757-3

For Worldwide Distribution, Printed in the U.S.A.

1 2 3 4 5 6 7 8 / 28 27 26 25 24

CONTENTS

INTRODUCTION

The greatest and noblest pleasure which we
have in this world is to discover new truths,
and the next is to shake off old prejudices.

—Frederick the Great,
King of Prussia 1740-1786

I grew up in Northern Ireland during the time of
"The Troubles," a civil war that ran from the late
1960s until Good Friday 1998. Car bombs, violent
kneecappings, terrorism, fear, and hatred were
almost inescapable. The deafening sound of the
bomb that was planted near my father's church,
and which decimated our town center, will always
live with me. The more gravesides that we each
stood beside, the harder it became for the nation to
forget—or to find a peaceful, forward movement.

I grew up in the Protestant, unionist tradition;
and because my father pastored a Protestant
church, it meant that our family was at the fore-
front not only of burying the dead but also needing
to make public comments to a congregation and

the wider community to help them process the terrible things happening all around them.

Due to the complete segregation of the education system, our divided communities, and our different leisure lives, I did not meet a Roman Catholic person until my mid-teenage years! Catholics and Protestants in Northern Ireland were very much sworn enemies and this played out through our politics as much as in our streets.

In their fight to "save" an Irish republic most Catholics would vote along nationalist, or "republican" lines, meaning they wanted Northern Ireland to separate from Britain and be united with the Republic of Ireland. And the Protestants would vote along "unionist" lines, meaning they wanted Northern Ireland to remain within the union with Great Britain. Religion, faith, and politics were never separated. You went to church to show which political side you were on. We never questioned it. You "saved" the nation by voting, and for many it was literally a matter of life and death.

At the same time, my husband, David, was growing up across the Irish Sea, in Scotland. His nation was becoming restless; grappling as to whether *it* should be independent from England and the rest of the United Kingdom. The Scottish

National Party was growing in influence toward a majority and a whole people were split down the middle, wrestling their future at the ballot box—for a harmonious unity of the nations, or for the responsibility of independent self-determination.

In the midst of this I was earning a politics degree at university and gave the best part of four years to thinking almost exclusively about the best structures and methods for healthy nations. Then one day God spoke to me and asked me to vote *opposite* to every political inclination I had—opposite to every deeply ingrained, culturally defined ideology that was within me and opposite to what I thought was best for a nation.

I remembered back to the death threats against my family when I was a child and the bloodthirstiness of my perceived human enemies and said to God, "Surely, Lord, You could not ask this of me?" Perplexed, yet yielded, and with many hours of asking God, "Why?" (and Him not responding), I stood; and despite my reservations, I voted opposite to every belief I'd ever held. I felt sick. But at that point God began speaking again and He said, *"Now* I can trust you with revelation about nations, because you have killed your personal preferences."

Obedience is thrilling, even when it churns your stomach, because you know you are submitting to a loving God who knows better than you.

OUR ASSIGNMENT

> *Then Jesus came to them and said, "All authority in heaven and on earth has been given to me. Therefore go and make disciples of all nations, baptizing them in the name of the Father and of the Son and of the Holy Spirit, and teaching them to obey everything I have commanded you. And surely I am with you always, to the very end of the age"* **(Matthew 28:18-20 NIV).**

Obedience is thrilling because you know you are submitting to a loving God who knows better than you.

In the clamor and press of busy lives we know that, as the people of God, we bear responsibility for the dissemination of the gospel, the discipling of nations, influencing culture, and crying out for the return of King Jesus. However, this can feel like an overwhelming assignment and how we do this is often unclear, especially when we face the ballot box at the polling station.

It is not always obvious how Jesus would think if He were standing in our shoes! Culture often cries more loudly than the Bible, our upbringing silently screams in our ears—an unidentified but ever-present soundtrack—and on occasions the teaching of men leads us more than the teaching of Jesus Christ does. If we're honest with ourselves, perhaps the kingdoms of this world and their glory pull at us more than the Kingdom of God.

TIME FOR HONEST REFLECTION

Our desire to "fix" things levers actions out of us that should require greater reflection before acting. It is a time to cogitate on how we think, and how we vote. We need to really ask ourselves how much we are really working *with* God in the extension of His Kingdom and conversely how much are we inadvertently pouring out our energies into the kingdoms of this world.

As people who love Jesus we need to ask honest questions of ourselves, such as:

- Does what I choose at the ballot box matter to God?
- How do I prioritize my responsibilities for the well-being of the nation?
- What should be the role of Holy Spirit-filled, prophetic people in the midst of our contemporary "culture wars"?

We now see the politicization of our faith infect righteous, biblical responsibility. Extreme nationalism—where our nation, our leaders, and our laws are exalted to the same level as the Kingdom of God, Jesus Christ, and Holy Scripture—is becoming ever more rampant, even in the church. It's becoming harder to separate the prophets from the political pundits, and nationalist ideologies are frequently mistaken for gospel truth. Some party political rallies look and sound like a Pentecostal service, while some church events feature more national flag waving than at an international soccer match! The lines are blurred.

As I write, and as you read, let me invite you to journey to review and reflect, and to allow ourselves to be challenged by the person of Jesus and the Scriptures, holding ourselves under a holy spotlight and letting our lives be scrutinized, so that we might have any impurities syphoned off. In this traveling together through these pages may we be collectively pierced, to think about the stewarding of nations and politics with a more robust mind—the mind of Christ.

THE CLASH OF THE KINGDOMS

Underpinning everything we consider must be this thought: The Kingdom of God is revolutionary and dangerous to all other powers. It may offend my current sensibilities. The Kingdom of God is an ever-expanding Kingdom. As the prophet writes, *"Of the increase of His government and peace there shall be no end"* (Isaiah 9:7 NKJV). God is always increasing His dominion through us, multiplying His impact with an unlimited growth. His royal power and impact on this earth will continue to immeasurably grow. We must expect to partner and work with the God who, at the core of His being and central to how He thinks, wants me to be successful in the fulfillment of His goal for His Kingdom to increase.

The Kingdom of God is revolutionary and dangerous to all other powers. It may offend my current sensibilities.

There is always a clash between the Kingdom of God and the kingdoms of this world—the kingdom of darkness. When Jesus was led into the wilderness by the Spirit of God to be tempted, satan offered Him the kingdoms of this world *"and their glory"* (Matthew 4:8 NASB). Satan does not just offer Jesus mere possessions—he offers worldly glory. There is a glory that can seduce you that is offered by satan, and we have developed an appetite for that false glory—for the adulation of people, for the positions of power as defined by them. We glory in scaling the heights of man-made structures, for the ways that mere humans think things should be fixed, and for a version of domination and impact that rules over us. And we like this journey. We tend to like a popular "prophetic" word that offers cheap, easy comfort, or a political "prophetic" word, having traded the glory of God for the glory of people.

THE KINGDOM OF GOD

The Kingdom of God is largely counterculture to the man-made ideals of the Western church and is totally subversive to the ways of humankind. Most of us are familiar with the concept of "kingdom" as it applies historically. We usually understand it in terms of military powers, such as the Roman Empire or the British Empire. These empires conquered and controlled by conquest and force, so it's easy to wrongly categorize the Kingdom of God as a dominating empire. When we conceive it like that, we wrongly think that rising to the top, and exercising top-down impact is how God's Kingdom works.

In fact, the Kingdom of God is deeply opposite to the satanically constructed thought processes we have. Remember, it is revolutionary and dangerous to all other powers. It is an offense and threat to these powers of the world. Of course, at its heart the Kingdom of God has a King with royal authority and power, and it does have (expanding) territorial boundaries (Isaiah 9:7) but the Kingdom of God is in the image of Jesus Christ so you cannot speak of it without understanding the nature of the Servant King it reflects. Yahweh God does not run a top-down subjugation and domination empire! Rather, He, being perfect love, is interested in liberation and the growth of His family, one soul at a time—every person matters to Him. The sending of His son, Jesus, to suffer and die to give access to this Kingdom shows that the blood of Christ liberates us into Kingdom belonging. The expanding territory of the Kingdom is measured not in square miles of land but by counting the hearts of sons and daughters who yield in faithful allegiance to the Good Father.

Yes, we *are* subject to a ruler, and it is vital that we understand we have a King who is Lord, however our King is good news to all people—and no other kingdom is fully good news. The Kingdom comes in demonstratable, measurable signs and wonders that illustrate the nature of the Creator King Himself. These wonders are that people get healed, lives are totally turned around, demons are exorcised, the hungry are fed, security in an eternal future is acquired, and sins are forgiven upon repentance. The Kingdom extends its boundaries, not by a land grab or national law change, but by the demonstration of God's rulership over sin, sickness, demons, and death.

The Kingdom of God is inherited by those who give up their rights to themselves.

There is no primogeniture or nepotism in the Kingdom of God—you don't inherit it based on a feudal ancestry system, passed down by right from father to firstborn son! Rather it comes to the childlike and those who give up their rights to themselves.

The King reigns within you, and His power indwells you. His dwelling—His habitation—is inside man and woman, those who answer and open the door to Him. It is worth giving up everything for. It is a joy to repeat this—the Kingdom of God is revolutionary and dangerous to all other powers! You do not enter His Kingdom by sliding in with no decision. No! Forceful people lay hold of it—not because they own and possess more things and titles, but because they liberate more people!

The kingdoms of this world only know top-down domination where they extend their boundaries by invasion, war, and conquering via military might, whereas the Kingdom of God is armed with power and authority in the Spirit so that you can liberate hearts and minds. Satan will always manipulate for his own ends, but overall the power of God is evidenced in changed, transformed lives.

The Kingdom of God does not tolerate performance, pretense, ego, territorialism, tyranny, freedom-as-defined-by-man (individual freedom to do whatever I want), human structures, politicization of the faith, or sharing glory. His Kingdom is always at war with anything that keeps God from His children; and the only way its citizens do great exploits is by knowing their God. It is more revolutionary than you have begun to see and it is not just about allegiance to Jesus and rule keeping—the Kingdom hates religious duty and obligation.

It does not need legislated freedom of speech to survive, it does not like a state that panders to it, it does not get in bed with lawmakers and weaponized nostalgia. It shakes nations to their foundations and provokes them into either the obedience or rejection of Jesus Christ. It sounds treasonous!

KINGDOM REVOLUTIONARIES

The gospel of the Kingdom of God calls the world to account and the world—including the religious—is forced to reckon with those who proclaim it. The Kingdom revolutionaries are being set apart and set on fire. The revolution of the Kingdom is here, the revolution of the Kingdom is now! Because the Kingdom of God sounds treasonous to every system and human structure, there will always be those who bark against you—it is part of the path. It is the sound that will accompany you if you are faithful to the Lord.

To fulfill your role in the body of Christ as a revolutionary, Kingdom forerunner, you will take a lot of hits, but you must be faithful to the Lord:

- We do not fight for a framework; we fight for a *relationship*.

- We do not fight for an organization; we fight for an *encounter*.

- We do not fight for a place at the table of men. Rather we step boldly before the throne of grace where we are always on a sure footing with the compassion and celebration of God.

We must stop training people to only survive within the traditional structures we have made, and to only fit the thing we are doing. Instead, we must equip people to know their God and to subvert the kingdoms of this world, rescuing people from them. So the call is to be curious, to create, to break things, to always ask why, to experiment, to understand that we are catalyzers but not always organizers.

The call to the Kingdom revolutionaries, under God, is to throw hand grenades, to challenge, to provoke, and to innovate. This means that you will need to be content in making mistakes on occasions, because at the core of the Kingdom revolutionary is a relationship that by instinct makes you *anti* the structure of the world. So if anyone fires you, you'll be the same Kingdom revolutionary and do it all again. While you keep asking questions about what the Kingdom of God should be, you will keep Jesus more central than your own anointing.

If you have loved the kingdoms of this world, no matter how long you have travelled in the wrong direction, you still have the chance to turn around.

PRAYER

Father God, I'm sorry where I have been slow to be obedient to You and dull of hearing because what You required seemed to be against my direction of travel. Jesus, help me hear You and yield to You—even if I do not understand and do not like it—for Yours is the Kingdom, the power, and the glory. Amen.

1

GOD SHAKES
THE WORLD

[Aslan] raised his head and roared, "Now it
is time!" then louder, "Time!"; then so loud
that is could have shaken the stars, "TIME!"

—C.S. Lewis,
The Chronicles of Narnia: The Last Battle

THE GOD WHO SHOCKS
THE EARTH

As a prophetic community, it is our responsibility
to understand the timings of God. We must know
the rhythms of Heaven, and where we are in the
story that God is telling on the earth. In this era,
in the second decade of the 21st century, we are
watching God shaking the world. Three powerful
translations of Isaiah 2:19 describe how the Lord:

- "*...rises to terrify the earth*" (NASB).

- "*...rises to shake the earth mightily*" (NKJV).
- "*...rises to make the earth tremble*" (NASB95).

This lends a biblical legitimacy to the sense that God frightens the earth to provoke humankind to make decisions toward Him. God does not move here to shake a single individual, but the totality of the human race—and all of nature is shuddering at this point in human history. God is harvest-ori-entated and puts thornbushes in our path, so we stretch to find Him. His wholly terrifying actions always have a redemptive plan within them.

Isaiah is clear to say that God "rises." That is unusual, because mostly in Scripture He is defined as *seated* on His throne (see Isaiah 6; Daniel 7). This indicates that His glory and also His judicial, fiery side is *moving* toward a sinful earth. This truth is given that we might under-stand the God who shocks the earth to throw it into a state resembling the chaos of its pre-creation beginning, that we may see that the only hope is Jesus. This means that we will see unusual and abnormal happenings in the days ahead on the

The human race is shuddering at this point in our history.

earth—earthquakes: physically; nationally; structurally; politically.

NATIONS FORCED TO CHOOSE

God's hand is at work in the nations, making them think about leadership and future desires. As I write this at the beginning of 2024, this year is being called the "year of the vote," where nations face great transformation—and not all of it good. Seven of the ten most populous nations of the world will go to the ballot box in 2024, and half the world's population will pick their politics or government. This will lead the earth into a number of years of calamity. We could call this the "Crisis Era."

In total, 64 nations are likely to hold elections this year, including:

United States of America	Pakistan
Bangladesh	Mexico
United Kingdom	Indonesia
India	Russia
Taiwan	El Salvador
Azerbaijan	Belarus
Senegal	Cambodia

Iran	Slovakia
Dominican Republic	South Africa
Rwanda	Mozambique
Romania	Croatia

Many of these votes are high-stakes elections and will push a tidal wave of thinking about what matters. After this year of voting will come a deepening of war on many continents, pushing the nations to keep searching and questioning. God is not letting up with world pressure anytime soon! None of this should surprise us as Jesus was very clear in Matthew 24 that these things were to come. The world's pundits are even asking the question, "Is democracy dying?"[1]

> **The world is asking, "WHO does freedom look like?"**

When surveyed, the younger generation (under 25) are indicating that they would be happy to surrender democracy in order to follow a dynamic, more dictatorial, "strong man" style of leadership. For them, democracy is not delivering! Globally, young people are giving up on democracy—perhaps because they are finding that, despite the world's advancements, they are not better off than their parents were.

We understand that the world is wrestling with its:

1. **Systems**
2. **History**
3. **Traditions**
4. **Values**

The nations rage and ask questions such as:

- "Do we have the framework of government we want?"
- "How do we rid ourselves of toxic history?"
- "Do we need to overturn traditions?"
- "Are our values sliding and becoming a prison for us?"

The great question the world is really asking is, "What does freedom look like?" Or better, *"Who* does freedom look like?"

The anti-Christ spirit has done a great, evil, multigenerational work of teaching toxic leadership to establish false definitions of freedom. Therefore, our nations labor under an illusion of what freedom is, and false governing ideologies teach the nations. Truly the nations have been led astray!

WHAT IS FREEDOM?

Most of us and our neighbors would probably define so-called "freedom" as having the ability to: be who I want to be; do what I want to do; earn what I want to earn; own what I want to own; identify as I want to be seen; choose as I want to choose; and to have my rights defined according to what makes *me* most comfortable.

There are of course more noble freedoms, such as freedom from poverty, freedom from tyranny, and freedom from slavery, but these get woven in among the demonically taught and inspired "freedoms." The world has been made into a prison for its inhabitants by satan, who has deceived us about freedom, and tied us up in the captivity of his values, his systems, his traditions, and *his* telling of our history. The battle lines are drawn!

Definitions of freedom *really* matter now. Ultimately—biblically—this is not about a political system. Instead, the truth is that:

- Freedom is being free from the law of sin and death.
- Freedom is being free from the captivity of sin and death.

- Freedom is being free from the structures of sin and death.

- Freedom is being free from the values of sin and death.

- Freedom is being free from the consequences of sin and death.

- Freedom is being free to be like Jesus Christ.

- Freedom is being free to conform to the image of Jesus.

- Freedom is being secure in your eternal destiny, with an understanding that you are first and foremost, before anything else, a citizen of the Kingdom of God.

Therefore, we must speak down the false freedom structures! Your leadership is now needed. You must become a mouthpiece of hope and begin to give Kingdom of God definitions of freedom. We understand that it is not "business as usual" and that right now many of us may be experiencing a nauseating, sick sensation, as the revelation dawns on us about what we have endured—and that we may still be in captivity, perhaps more than we realized. The Spirit of the Lord says:

> You will become megaphones of freedom and hope, and I will give

you a peculiar anointing of visibility in communication, but you *must* turn away from petty infighting, heresy hunting, and destructive, civil war tendencies that turn inwardly in the body of Christ. For your leadership must now speak outwardly beyond your current communication boundaries. I call you into outward-looking communication.

This is a time of crossover broadcasting and crossover relationships—crossing over the boundaries of the church and into significant places where leadership is in despair, where social commentators do not know how to encourage people, speaking freedom and hope. This is not the restoration of the structures, nor the restoration of traditions, but is the building properly into lives the hope and freedom of the Kingdom of God.

Do not agree with the status quo that speaks accusation, holds offense, and lives with a mindset to put people on trial. Rather, sing the songs of tomorrow; sing the songs of our future, and tell the stories of the plans of Jesus.

The world does not know its future. The church *does* know the future. This is your distinctive! Do not engage with the argumentative tendencies that you find in the modern church. Stop, turn, and speak hope.

In the name of Jesus, I bless you to speak the words, write the messages, and even compose the songs that reorientate people to true freedom in Jesus.

SHAKING FALSE IDOLS— SYSTEMS FAILURE

We see in the book of Jeremiah a blueprint for how God deals with wayward nations who find their security in systems that are not of Him: *"Where then are the gods you made for yourselves?"* (Jeremiah 2:28 NIV).

God is going to question the validity and strengths of what we have put in place to protect us (false gods). I see that from 2024 onward is the beginning of a great falling of false idols, which will take us

We must speak down the false freedom structures!

into world systems failure. While you might cheer at first hearing this, bear in mind that it is a sobering prophecy because it means that there will be economic collapses and judgment on some currencies, along with judiciaries making decisions that we will know are not just. God loves the world enough to shake and expose its errors—including within the House of God—that we may cry, "You alone, Jesus, are worthy! Lord, You alone are the way, the truth, and the life."

God will challenge how a nation secures itself, even through the alliances it makes:

"First here, then there—you flit from one ally to another asking for help. But your new friends in Egypt will let you down, just as Assyria did before" (Jeremiah 2:36 New Living Translation)."

Another translation puts it as: *"How unstable you are, constantly changing your ways! You will be put to shame by Egypt just as you were put to shame by Assyria* (Holman Christian Standard Bible)."

Although this verse pertained to Jerusalem when first written, the principles go beyond Judah's historic borders and into our current world. Today God is testing international alliances and looking at the righteousness of their foundational agreements. When nations make partnerships, we must be able to ask, "Did God catalyze this?" "Does He bless it?" and, "Is it itself protectionism without God?" When the nations throw off serious thoughts about God, God shows His displeasure with their newfound confidences, and He does not let them prosper in these alliances.

Nations can be ingenious in finding ways to guard themselves, even running to make agreement with multiple allies that, in doing so, dethrone God as leader, protector, and the first place that the nation goes to for its future to be secured. Therefore, we can expect to see international coalitions of nations not holding. The hope a nation puts in another nation will be shaken if they have taken God out of the equation. We will see God dealing with long-standing sin in nations' false foundational alliances. Allies will give trouble instead of help and this will open the door for conflict. When the covenants the world forms exclude God, they do not hold. The Lord has indicated we are to expect, "seismic movement."

I looked in the Spirit and saw stalemate in the United Nations (UN), with uncharacteristic aggression across debating chambers, and curses uttered by high-ranking officials in public, as ally turned against ally. I looked again and saw the

The hope a nation puts in another nation will be shaken if they have taken God out of the equation. North Atlantic Treaty Organization (NATO) flounder, with tremorous, cataclysmic cracks appearing in its foundations, leading nations to retreat from each other. Once more I looked and saw the Economic Community of West African States (ECOWAS) not able to stop the rise of fracturing and coups. In the redemptive purposes of God, He is making us acknowledge that the world has few answers to its future without Him.

THE WORLD CONTRACTS INTO SILOS

We've already looked at Isaiah 2:19, the Lord *"rises to terrify the earth."* The preceding verse describes men going to hide in caves and holes in the ground. They find the small place in the days of the demonstrations of God shaking the earth. They retreat into silos and what they perceive to be small agreements. This hyperlinks to another Scripture, Proverbs 28:2 (NIV): *"When a country is rebellious, it has many rulers"* [*many are its heads*] (Young's Literal Translation).

The world will contract into factions and splinter groups, siloing into smaller parties and narrowing opinions. Petty tyrants will arise, with the hasty elevation of self-protectionism and the rise of territorial small-mindedness. From 2024 onward the world will cry for retribution, and retaliation will become the soundtrack for many in this age.

I believe that the world is becoming the most dangerous place that it has been for generations, and we must watch and guard against small-minded, parochial thinking in the media that we consume. Know that the choices at the ballot box will not always be allowed to bring solutions. Watch the world bereft, because of its solution-less state. Yet in the middle of this the Lord says, "Let your joy be evident. For you are not swayed by the rumblings of the kingdoms of this world."

PRAYER

Lord Jesus, I desire that the joy of my salvation would be evidenced in my life. [As you pray this to Him, lay hands on your tummy and in His name command joy arising and a flow of joy that you may be a sign and a wonder in the nations.]

NOTE

1. BBC Radio 4 "Today Podcast," January 11, 2024.

2

WAR AND HARVEST

OVER-VIOLENCE IS NOT BACKED BY GOD

Many have debated over the years if there is any such thing as a "just war" and have asked, "Does the end justify the means?" In other words, do the consequences of making war justify entering it in the first place? Our starting point must be to ask prayerful questions of the Lord and not make a single assumption. We should ask questions including:

- "Is this conflict man-made?"
- "Is this conflict allowed by God?"
- "Is God allowing this war because of the consequences of sin over many years?"
- "Has God initiated anything here, or are we simply walking out the effects of humanity's inhumanity?"

I would seek to ask God for His redemptive purposes before I asked Him what side He was on.

One repetitive idea that we find time and again in the Bible is that God is *not* pleased with over-violent responses. Today we might call these, at their most extreme, war crimes, or genocide, but the bar may be lower.

> *But a prophet of the Lord named Oded was there, and he went out to meet the army* [Israel] *when it returned to Samaria. He said to them, "Because the Lord, the God of your ancestors, was angry with Judah, he gave them into your hand. But you have slaughtered them in a rage that reaches to heaven. And now you intend to make the men and women of Judah and Jerusalem your slaves. But aren't you also guilty of sins against the Lord your God? Now listen to me! Send back your fellow Israelites you have taken as prisoners, for the Lord's fierce anger rests on you"* **(2 Chronicles 28:9-11 NIV).**

Yahweh's fierce anger rests on nations who overuse violence, even in a war context. Watch our weeping Savior show anger to those who slaughter in a rage, irrespective of what side they are on.

Yahweh's fierce anger rests on nations who overuse violence, even in a war context.

SHAKING IS KEY FOR SALVATIONS

In the midst of this scene-setting for the next era, we stand on the rock of Jesus Christ and remember that God is, by default, *redemptive*. He is the One who makes all things new, and we anticipate a new Heaven and new earth, with the promise of a day of no more mourning, crying, or pain, when the old order of things passes away. We must only see what is happening within the context of mass harvest and salvations. The provocation of God is for His people to run to Him and is to frustrate the ways of the world. Therefore, harvest will never be easier than it is about to become!

I heard the Lord speak of our forgotten "harvesting abilities"—that we have soul-winning history, with international reach. The Spirit went on to say that we had spoken about evangelism and even trained for evangelism but had not harvested many souls. There has been a distraction where we've preferred methods over fruit, but

We must only see what is happening within the context of mass harvest and salvations. now God is releasing an ability to get in time with harvest.

Truly we are in the days of Zechariah 8:23, "*many will take hold of you, even from all the nations, because they will have heard God is with you.*" The year 2024 starts a journey of the great turning, which will be evidenced by an exponential growth in the numbers of new believers around the globe. It is not merely a day to propose that war is coming, but also to receive prophetic words and strategies that show us how to handle the well-being of nations.

I have heard God talk about us being a new resistance army, even as evil re-awakens in our midst. Undoubtedly in previous world conflicts the church was slow to move out from inadvertently (or even deliberately) backing evil, into being a force that terrified evil. We have not always been a military-minded church who knew how to go into the spirit realm and tear down, through spiritual warfare, the strongholds of bloodthirstiness and hate.

We are told to "know the wiles of the enemy." Look! The enemy has re-awakened a tidal wave of antisemitism and fascism (right-wing totalitarian regimes—a wrong definition of what pure people look like).

WHAT IS FASCISM?

We increasingly see stories about clashes between "fascist" and "anti-fascist" groups on our news programs; though since World War II few political parties would dare call themselves fascist, it tends to be used as an insult by their opponents. Nevertheless, elements of fascism appear to be on the rise in countries around the globe. Fascism is a political ideology (see also the Special Note in Chapter 11 for more about ideologies) that emerged in Italy (under Mussolini), then Germany (under Hitler and the Nazis) in the early half of the 20th century. A fascist government would be on the far-right of the usual left-right political spectrum and fascists are very nationalistic, led by strong, authoritarian, populist leaders.

Fascism's extreme authoritarian, nationalistic, and militaristic ideology usually manifests in a belief in racial purity (like the Nazi's idea of a "master race") and so fascist groups today are often identified by their racist and discriminatory language and behavior against minority ethnic groups, Jews, and immigrants.

Extremist ideologies like this usually rise in popularity during times of global shaking and upheaval, when people become suspicious or threatened by their neighbors, and their extreme nationalism leads to fearful protectionism, and then descends into violent fascism.

There is an urgent requirement for many to hear the Lord as He speaks nations into your heart again, and for you to find your passport, have your suitcase on standby, and obediently go start crusades of harvest! There is a strategy that God is giving to reduce the impact of evil—it requires us securing a tipping point of harvest in nations right now, so that there are new Christians in each land raised as military-minded (spiritually speaking) *ecclesia*, who can push back what satan is planning.

This is not the time to think about building your own barns. Rather, it is a time to go from house to house, and nation to nation, being a solution for the continents of the world, turning hearts to

Christ to minimize the destruction and spread of the coming wars.

Do you hear? God is releasing both an urgency right now in your spirits, as well as a fresh harvesting strategy. He is handing out "call up" conscription papers, and summoning you, that you would go. Stand, and hear Him speak about countries and how you will best reap harvest in them.

PRAYER

Father, forgive me for being ineffective in harvest. I confess that I have concerned myself with building and filling my own barns and storehouses and have forgotten the great commission that your Son gave me, to go into the world and make disciples. Renew your zeal in me again, remind me where my harvest field is.

Lord, I open my ears and my spirit to hear Your call, and to dream again. I stand up and shake all ineffective harvesting from my body. Jesus, I receive from You now a scythe in my hand, as a sign in the spirit of the harvest capabilities that You want to give me in this era of shaking. I choose to not lose focus of what is important to You in the midst of all that shakes, breaks, and rages in the days ahead. You are the God of redemption, give me Your heart for the harvest! In Jesus's name, amen.

3

WARTIME PROPHETS AND SATAN'S STRATEGY

For some years now I have read through the Bible twice every year. If you picture the Bible to be a mighty tree and every word a little branch, I have shaken every one of these branches because I wanted to know what it was and what it meant.

—Martin Luther,
Luther's Works, Vol. 54, "Table Talk," 165

THE REVELATION 11 MANDATE

As we grasp the sober and serious understanding of what is happening in the nations, we turn to Scripture to understand *how* and *who* God is raising up to lead in His name, at this hour. How does a wartime church need to think? What are the biblical expectations for the people of God in a time of war?

Jeremiah emphasizes the continual succession of prophets who diligently became the voice of God, in order that His thinking, solutions, and even His emotional status can unfailingly, undeniably, be known in a nation:

> Since the day that your fathers came out of the land of Egypt until this day, I have even sent to you all My servants the prophets, daily rising up early and sending them (Jeremiah 7:25 NKJV).

So when a nation is in crisis God always sends them a prophetic voice. When clarity and timings are needed, God raises those up with a passion for revelation, those who will push into seeing, hearing, and understanding in the Spirit. He gives the people prophets who are Spirit-filled but also demonstrate Spirit-led lives; those who have married wisdom and revelation.

When a nation is in crisis God always sends them a prophetic voice.

The Lord's ultimate desire for His people is that they are a prepared bride, spotless, and made ready. Revelation chapter 11 steps into this and delivers understanding on the core instinct of God's end-time church, and it is that *they prophesy.* The whole chapter outlines a church that is marked, moved, and stewarding—to great effect—the word of God.

The prophecy is safeguarded by those who are purified (more on this later). This remnant, end-time church is competent with heavenly revelation and has a disposition toward bravery and an urge to say exactly what God wants said. God is pulling on *your* life and leading you into this Revelation 11 place. You did not go through what you went through to stop now! He needs your purified voice.

> *I was given a reed like a measuring rod and was told, "Go and measure the temple of God and the altar, with its worshipers"* **(Revelation 11:1 NIV).**

The chapter begins with an instruction about measuring the temple. This metaphor is seen several times in the Old and New Testaments[1] and indicates that God is taking care of something to preserve it from destruction, to get it ready. God is preserving a people to prophesy!

> *...They will trample on the holy city for 42 months. And I will appoint my two*

witnesses, and they will prophesy for 1,260 days, clothed in sackcloth (**Revelation 11:2-3 NIV**).

John continues to write down what he is being told, now giving a time frame numbering 1,260 days[2] (which is 42 months), indicating a divinely allotted, and protected, time period when God's people will have to speak revelation. These verses announce to us that God has preserved and equipped a people so they are fully ready to enter a time where they will prophesy and speak out the word of God. *You* are part of this. *You* have been preserved to bring uncontaminated revelation! In the days of the cataclysmic clash of the kingdoms, God raises an end-times prophetic church.

THE ENEMY'S BATTLE PLAN— HOW SATAN LEADS

Revelation chapter 11 and Daniel chapter 7 appear to note similar periods of time. While Revelation 11 talks of the role of end-times church to prophesy, Daniel 7 gives insight into what will come against this church. Verse 25 is packed with prophetic insight into how our adversary will specifically target us to lead us astray and into his kingdom, rather than toward the Kingdom of God:

> *He* [our enemy, the antichrist or satan] *shall speak words against the Most High, and shall wear out the saints of the Most High, and shall think to change the times and the law; and they shall be given into his hand for a time, times, and half a time* (Daniel 7:25 ESV).

First: Words of Accusation

First, accusation will be the major battle of the days ahead: *"He shall speak words against the Most High..."* (Daniel 7:25 ESV). Satan plans to speak against the saints of the Most High—stirring up pain, reputational damage, misunderstanding, defensiveness, and infighting—all because he will accuse falsely. Beware—when prophetic people have undealt-with emotions because they've been on the receiving end of maligning, it pollutes their revelation!

The most outlandish and yet successful approach in the face of accusation is to quote Isaiah to your inner world, saying, *"like a sheep before its shearers is silent,*"[3] "I have no need to defend my reputation." When this truth has deeply medicated your inner world and you understand that your defensiveness achieves nothing (and neither does fighting for your own reputation) you are able to turn and produce the purified word of the Lord.

Prayer

Savior Jesus, help me be more like You. I strengthen myself in the knowledge that Your love and acceptance of me is sufficient, and that I do not need to fight back against accusation and slander. Lord, I trust You to bring justice, as and when you feel it is right, in your infinite wisdom. I let go of every sense and emotion of injustice that I have grasped tightly to myself and I choose to release it into Your hands. Following the example of You, Jesus, I choose now to forgive all those who have accused me, misunderstood me, slandered me, gossiped about me, or spoken ill of me, whether to my face or behind my back. Lord, I am sorry for partnering with offense and for desiring to defend myself. Holy Spirit, help me to be patient, self-controlling, and peaceful in this, even though it is painful. My God, I trust You. You are my defender, and You are the One who restores me. Thank You for Your mercy and grace. Amen.

Second: He Will Exhaust You

Second, satan will try to exhaust you and wear you out: *"...and shall wear out the saints of the Most High..."* (Daniel 7:25 ESV). To stand in, and with, the word of the Lord requires strength, and an ability to bear its weight. Considering that the exhaustion will come from the demonic spirit realm, it is battled against by Spirit-led decrees that banish any atmosphere of weariness from around you.

Decree

In the mighty name of Jesus Christ, I forbid any demonic atmosphere of exhaustion and weariness to hang over me anymore. I eject them from my world; and in their place, I receive the zeal of the Lord to accomplish what He has given to me!

The most successful approach in the face of accusation is to realize that you have no need to defend your reputation.

Third: He Will Change Your Timings

Third, satan will try to change the timings. "...*and shall think to change the times...*" (Daniel 7:25 ESV). (Other Bibles translate these as the *"set times"* or *"sacred seasons"*), thus pushing you out of being able to bring revelation that is on time and effective. A consistent awareness of this is now required in your life so you can bless your thinking, speaking, geography, and relationships to be in the timing of God.

If you can't keep in time, you will not lead or speak the words of the Lord in season. Rather, you will find yourself bringing out-of-date revelation, frustrating yourself and being inadequate to those who need detailed specifics in the coming days of shaking and war.

Prayer

Ask God if there are any hindrances to your keeping pace and being in sync with Him. Is there any disobedience or wrong connections that pull you out of time? Allow the Spirit of God to hover over you, bringing you back into the rhythm of the Lord at this time. If the enemy has really lied to you and your decision making is not in step with God, ask Him to "magnetize" you by the renewing of your mind back to truth and into good decision making.

Fourth: Setting Unrighteous Laws

Finally, satan will try to set unrighteous laws. *"He... shall think to change...the law..."* (Daniel 7:25 ESV). These laws are not just national governmental edicts, but the demonic laws of control, territorial thinking, religious behavior boundaries, and false hierarchical structures in the church that allow for spiritual abuse.

This calls for you to love the Kingdom of God and understand how it operates so you can discern between a godly Kingdom value and a kingdom-of-this-world value. A Kingdom principle versus a demonic principle. The dominant state of most of the church is that we walk as "natural" rather than spiritual people. Our spirits and flesh are not dominated and in submission to the Spirit of God; therefore things *of* the Spirit jar against us, or do not sit well with us.

This is why those who prophesy often get much kickback to their revelation, because many listeners think with only their natural mind and so do not have the capability to receive the words of the

Spirit. Instead, sadly, they become offended and walk away, disregarding or rejecting revelation.

Our lives have been crafted by natural means and fleshly values—for example by the films we watch, our education systems, and our news media—which often block us to the ways of the Spirit of God, like wearing sunglasses in an already dark room. In Jesus's conversation with Nicodemus in John 3,[4] He says that unless we are born again, we cannot see the Kingdom of God. This is not just a future statement of what is available to you in eternity! Rather, once you are saved you have the ability to spiritually see—to perceive with inward spiritual perception, to experience the culture and values of the Kingdom of God.

You must discern between a godly Kingdom value and a kingdom-of-this-world value.

We have ebbed and flowed and not stayed in connection with the Spirit, or stayed in encounter with the Spirit, and so we are not really in the realm of being those who *live* by the Spirit. How therefore would we know how to discern between what the Holy Spirit is doing versus what the demonic spirits of the age are doing?

Paul is quite brutal in how he writes to the Corinthian church in his first letter to them. He says to an entire gathered Christian community, *"I could not address you as people who live by the Spirit but as people who are still worldly"* (1 Corinthians 3:1 NIV). Paul could not talk to them about spiritual matters because they had fallen short of understanding the ways of the Spirit.

SPIRITUAL DISCERNMENT

To safeguard against unrighteous laws, values, and culture you must pray to delineate and discern between what is flesh and what is Spirit. This will immediately take you to understand what is the culture of the Kingdom versus when satan is really in charge. So much of what we do in church is nervous, fleshly energy and has very little to do with the Holy Spirit or the Kingdom of God. If our churches are not dominated by the Holy Spirit and we have not even fully recognized this, why would we in turn expect to understand what satan is doing in the culture of nations?

You must pray urgently that the Spirit of God would fill you, lead you, and dominate you, so that you are a carrier of God's Kingdom and a high-level discerner of the difference between the Kingdom

To safeguard against unrighteous laws, values, and culture, you must pray to delineate and discern between what is flesh and what is Spirit.

of God and the false, worldly kingdom of satan. Then—and only then—will you be able to truly see where satan has led. When we have overcome what seeks to derail us, the aim is that we become prophetic voices who stand before the "Lord of the earth," having power in the heavenly realms and the atmosphere, over the waters of the earth and over the land.

THE POWER OF PURIFIED END-TIMES PROPHETS

Revelation 11 speaks of the impact of the purified, prophetic end-times church: fire will come from their mouths; they will shut up the heavens and control weather patterns; they will travel with the Holy Spirit to where God sits and rules. They are the "come up here" revelators, who prophesy from the heights of God's perspective.

"And I will appoint my two witnesses, and they will prophesy for 1,260 days,

clothed in sackcloth." They are "the two olive trees" and the two lamp-stands, and "they stand before the Lord of the earth." If anyone tries to harm them, fire comes from their mouths and devours their enemies. This is how anyone who wants to harm them must die. They have power to shut up the heavens so that it will not rain during the time they are prophesying; and they have power to turn the waters into blood and to strike the earth with every kind of plague as often as they want (Revelation 11:3-6 NIV).

These prophetic people—exemplified by the two witnesses—are modeled on the life of Moses and Elijah. They will steward the world at the end of time and they have a responsibility to deal with sin and judgment, with strong messages of repentance. They will command international atmospheres. They *do* face persecution and death—theirs is not an easy job. This is the kind of prophetic community that will understand what it is to follow in the footsteps of Jesus, our suffering Master.

With great care I suggest that we are now attempting to lay foundations for a generation of prophets who will occupy this space. They will go from glory to glory, and from faith to faith. Right now we may have elements of this, but we are not yet fully formed to occupy this biblical description of the church.

The journey we are on *matters*, because we are obliged to become those who:

- Understand our biblical call and function.
- Tremble with reverential fear of the Lord at the authority and words He will give us.
- Understand that the prophets do not scrap and fight in the kingdoms of this world, but instead prophesy, from beside and inside of God, over the nations of the world.

These prophets will show the higher power of God, but also the consequences of sin.

NOTES

1. For examples, Zechariah 2:1-5 and Revelation 21:15-17.

2. We know from Daniel 7 and 12 that this time signifies a length of persecution of God's people. John's revelation could refer literally to a 42-month period of tribulation that is still to come in the future or might simply refer more symbolically to the time between Jesus's first and second comings—an epoch when most believers around the world are under great pressure and persecution from the nations. I believe a third option— that both interpretations are true—we are in-between, but there is end-time tribulation to come. These verses are therefore incredibly relevant for us, today.

3. Isaiah 53:7.

4. John 3:3 (NIV): *"Jesus replied, 'Very truly I tell you, no one can see the kingdom of God unless they are born again.'"*

4

KINGDOM-THINKING CITIZENS

The seeking of the kingdom of God is
the chief business of the Christian life.

—Jonathan Edwards,
"Great Awakening" Revivalist

WHAT IS
THE KINGDOM OF GOD?

Throughout this book you will read continual
mention of a concept called the "Kingdom of
God" (KOG) aka the "Kingdom of Heaven."
While Isaiah prophesied the coming Messiah,
Daniel was more concerned with predicting the
coming KOG, beginning when he interpreted a
dream of Nebuchadnezzar (a statue representing
the kingdoms of this world was smashed by a
rock): *"the God of heaven will set up a kingdom
that will never be destroyed, nor will it be left to*

another people. It will crush all those kingdoms and bring them to an end, but it will itself endure forever" (Daniel 2:44 NIV).

By AD 27, Jews were eagerly expecting this new kingdom age, a time when Heaven and earth would be once again united (as they were in the Garden), and the whole earth would be filled with the knowledge of God's glory—an epoch when everything that rebels against God's reign is defeated and washed away, and the King's will is done on earth, just as it is in Heaven.

Just then, Jesus began to preach His core message that, "Good news! The Kingdom of God is here!" The long-awaited Kingdom had been inaugurated and was—is—right here, right now.

However, it wasn't quite as simple as it sounds. First-century Jews expected that this would look like a worldly power, a strong, nationalistic, geographical, and undeniably physical presence on the global stage. Then, as the centuries progressed, Jesus's followers begin to similarly think that the increasingly powerful and structured church was equal to the Kingdom. But Jesus and

His apostles never used the words Kingdom and church interchangeably!

The KOG is uniquely spiritual, more like another dimension that exists alongside our own. Jesus broke the curse of evil, sin, chaos, and death, that creation sat under. Now, like Spring arriving in the frozen wastes of Narnia, we see ever-growing evidence of the KOG. Some of its signposts are deliverances, healings, signs, wonders, miracles, and salvations. The KOG expands because Jesus has gone to the Father, and it manifests in us, and through us.

One day, Jesus will return to renew the earth and re-unite it with Heaven. Until then we live with the paradox that the KOG is both *now* and yet also *not yet!*

WE ARE TO BE REVOLUTIONARY FORERUNNERS

Good news friend! God is leading us away from being a reactionary, stagnant church structure and transforming us into a revolutionary, forerunning church movement.

- We are shifting away from the days of defensive commentary, protective punditry, and stubborn maintenance of the church's *status quo*, and into a speaking ahead of the curve about the changing epochs with words that are transformative to people.

- We, the *ecclesia* of God, are to be engaged in prophetically signposting and constructing the future and serving the people, and their lands, into transformative change.

- We will shift from only being able to remark, unhelpfully, that "one day everything will change" (which is the rhetoric of stating the obvious!), as we now step into our true forerunning call, which resists the kingdoms of this world, and leads with words and decrees that reframe with a Kingdom perspective and set things in a heavenly order.

- We will end our partnership with fear that has kept us quiet for too long—a fearful silence that tolerated grave, sinful errors—just in case people would reject us.

- We will understand that maintaining godly integrity and boldly forth-telling revelation will often risk our reputation.

With the rise of war, intense shakings, and God terrifying the earth, but also great harvest and a purified prophetic church that leads the way, we need mindsets that are prepared for the future, not stuck in the shock of a moment. The contemporary prophetic movement has caused many to turn and jeer at prophets because of a host of inaccurate words that left people scrabbling around for clarity. Our inability to take ownership of the words only further compounded our reputational demise in many circles, both within and without the church.

Perhaps our so-called "revelation" has merely demonstrated that those of us who claimed to prophesy have been living more as citizens of the world than of Heaven. Especially—and this has been really painful over the last few years—we have been exposed as having been preoccupied with our own nations, more than we have been captivated and transfixed by the Kingdom of Christ Jesus!

Consequently, it is not unusual to find prophetic words being released that mis-create reality. What

I mean by this is that trusted leaders in the body of Christ have a positional authority that molds how those under their care and influence see the world. So, when these leaders and prophets misspeak, their words become their followers' reality.

Prophetic people, let me tell you, if we are not fully in the Kingdom in our thinking, then we mislead and mis-assign hope—arguing from inside the world and therefore far from the truth of how the Kingdom actually works!

Perhaps those of us who claimed to prophesy have been living more as citizens of the world than of Heaven, preoccupied with our own nations rather than captivated by the Kingdom of God.

We must be really honest with ourselves: have we have become so determined to defend the places we have secured for ourselves, the reputations that we have built for ourselves, and the righteous opinions that we think we must have, that we have become partially blind to the story that the Kingdom of God is outworking? In that atmosphere our prophetic words and visions can *sound* and *look* plausible—and we may truly believe that they are from

Have we have become so determined to defend our security, reputation, and our opinion that we have become blind to the story that the Kingdom of God is outworking?

God—but they have come from the atmosphere of the world, rather than carrying the weight of the substance of another realm entirely—the Kingdom of God.

Therefore, it is imperative that "Kingdom of God Truth-Tellers" emerge in this hour! More than ever, it is vital that we discover what and how God thinks about things—*especially nations, politics, and justice*—so that the church can better reflect Him in its compassion and in its transformative, Spirit-filled power.

PRAYER

Jesus, I repent of all the times when I am reactionary, defensive, and easily offended. Would You lift off me all the weight of trying to justify before men and women things that I do not need to protect and defend. By this confession to You, I release myself of this burden and acknowledge that You are Lord, You are true justice, and You do not need me to fight these battles. I want to live not being so easily triggered. Jesus, would You put on me Your mindset, that of a forerunner who knows how to think revolutionary thoughts and who resists the comfort of the moment. I want to be a useful voice to steer people into the future. Lord, my life is Yours! Amen.

5

BIBLICAL NATIONHOOD

No nation can have a monopoly on God…

—Pastor John Hagee

HOW DOES GOD THINK ABOUT NATIONS?

There is so much to be gleaned from Scripture that will help us answer this question. But some of what we will discover as we explore the Bible might poke at, provoke, or even disrupt some of what we have previously thought—or assumed—is in God's plan and on His heart for nations. Shall we pray and agree together that, as we wash ourselves in truth, let all that is not scriptural be removed from us! The concepts that follow must be clearly defined from the outset, not as *biblical national-ism*, but *biblical nationhood*. The importance for this nuanced difference will become apparent.

God believes in nations; He established Israel with clear, distinctive boundaries. Much of the words of the law and prophets of the Old Testament is about maintaining the cultural and social distinction of the people of Israel from the surrounding, pagan nations. National identity, national distinctiveness, and national cultures matter. The tribes of Israel were divinely separated and constructed to be ethnically different from their neighbors.

Job said of God that, *"He builds up nations, and He destroys them. He expands nations, and He abandons them"* (Job 12:23 New Living Translation). God is either found in the business of raising up nations or of punishing—even abandoning—them. When we look at the historic and contemporary journeys of nations we might ask as prophets, according to this verse, "Is God building up, expanding, and blessing here? Or is God diminishing, punishing, or even in the process of abandoning?" If we prophetically sense that the nation is being diminished by God, how He does it is found in the following verse: *"He deprives the leaders of the earth of their reason; he makes them wander in a trackless wasteland"* (Job 12:24).

If your country's leader is lacking good judgment, unable to gather and appeal to the people,

A nation usually gets the leader it deserves. has lost the confidence of the wise, is wandering in circular, unhelpful ways (perhaps with a sense of contracted or wilderness-type economics), and has no good solutions, then you know God is teaching the nation a lesson by depriving the leaders of reason. The nation usually gets the leader it deserves.

Confusion is given to nations—along with an ever-increasing uncertainty in conditions. In those instances, we see courage failing, leaders develop self-infatuation, and we witness distracted council chambers in government, more interested in infighting and bipartisan squabbles than the actual business of leading a people. It is worth taking time to meditate on this verse in Job 12:24 and see if it is being outworked in your own land.

Perhaps the most significant set of verses in scripture around biblical nationhood are found in Acts 17, where Paul tells the Athenian philosophers that:

> *From one man* [alternate translations cite the words "blood" (NKJV) or "ancestor" (NRSV)] *he* [God] *made all the nations, that they should inhabit*

the whole earth; and he marked out their appointed times in history and the boundaries of their lands. God did this so that they would seek Him and perhaps reach out for him and find him, though he is not far from any one of us (Acts 17:26-27 NIV).

God established national boundaries to help humankind find God. Nations are formed missiologically—the study of the church's mission—to find Jesus. Consequently, I believe that each nation carries certain attributes of the character of God, different ways for how they reflect Him and show Him off to others, specific means by which they see Him, and distinct ways that they find Him. Nations recognize God in different ways, especially as God creates landmasses to look dissimilar and distinctive.

And the people who live in these places are wired to find God according to ethnic temperament and national topography—in other words, they recognize God in different attributes of the creation around them. The people of the Arctic are wired to find God in a frozen, barren desert. The people of the equator are wired to find God in brilliant heat and sunshine. Nevertheless, it is only a partial recognition: each nation brings their insights of God to the table. Ergo, for our own nations we should be able to divulge to one another our distinctives.

- What aspect of God does your nation bring to the table?
- What aspect of God is reflected in the landscape of your nation?
- What aspect of God is reflected in your cultural distinctives?
- What aspect of God is reflected in your cultural values?

If I were to come to your nation, what would I learn about God from spending time in your landscape, watching your people, and learning about your shared identity? Therefore, we do not visit other nations to "put them right." Rather we should humbly seek to learn more of the character and nature of the Creator in our encounters with foreigners; in turn, they will study our lives, gaining insight into how our local culture sees and understands Yahweh.

The verses we just read in Acts 17 immediately follow on from Paul standing in Athens pointing to an altar with the inscription, "To An Unknown

God." In essence, Paul says to the people, "Look how imperfect your recognition of God has been—you don't even know the name of your God!" Likewise, our own nations are prone to say, with their secularist agenda, there is no God here, we don't reflect Him. But Paul goes on to declare that God is near, *"God did this so that they would seek him and perhaps reach out for him and find him, though he is not far from any one of us"* (Acts 17:27 NIV). (This should help answer the age-old question of, "How will God judge people who have never had a missionary preach the gospel?" He will judge in accordance with how the people recognize or find God in the fabric of their nation!)

GOD SETS THE TIMES OF NATIONS

We find as we focus in on verse 26 of Acts 17, that God "sets times in nations." Other translations suggest that He has marked out their:

- *"appointed times in history"*
- *"exact times and their limits"*
- *"when they rise and fall"*

Let's look at this positively: God blesses nations to rise in order to show off specific attributes of Himself. His glory is displayed in those times. For example, from the Romans we learned about constructing society, law, and order. From the Celtic tribes and lands we gained a wild impulsiveness and storytelling. From the Italians we discover the pleasures of art and music. From the Greeks we wonder at the beauty of human bodies—and minds; we track the wonders of science and mathematics. From China, we see God reflected through a land of honor and community. From the Israelites we gain healthy, Hebraic thinking, where the spiritual and natural realms interweave. And so on—specific gifts that reflect the character of God are given to each ethnic group in their moments of time.

Appointed seasons of leadership ebb and flow, and even a time of preeminence on the world stage is permitted, according to what the world needs to focus on with regard to the attributes of Christ. Each race is called to play its part in the drama of world history. God sets their prosperity, their rises, and their falls, and He limits their borders.

In the days of my great grandparents, the British Empire still stretched from where the sun rose over the Pacific, across the vast continent of Asia, parts of Africa, and even touched the shores of America. For a little over a century, it was "the greatest Empire the world has ever seen." For good and for ill, it ushered in the Industrial Age of invention and global expansion.

God blesses nations to rise in order to show off specific attributes of Himself.

And yet, within a generation—and two world wars—it was all over, its economy in tatters, its industry overtaken by younger, modern powers, and its colonial domination broken into independent nation states. The British Empire went the way of the Roman, Greek, Ottoman, Mongol, Qing, Babylonian, Assyrian, and Egyptian, just as in Nebuchadnezzar's dream.

God has given sufficient limits and resources to each nation and expects them to refrain from invasion, domination, empire mindsets, and dictatorship. I believe we can confidently say that in the main wars of empire are therefore evil—we do not plunder and rob a nation of its God-given attributes in the world by enforcing our own on them.[1]

THE TRUE WEALTH OF NATIONS

You *do* need to love where God has birthed you, and the attributes of the nation you carry are unique elements of your heavenly Father. Even if you do not live in the nation of your birth, you will always carry some part of how it is supposed to display God's glory.[2] These attributes should be beautifully liberating: what is considered statesman-like in Northern Ireland is not what is considered statesman-like in the Netherlands or the USA. And that is okay.

All nations have wealth because God has marked out their times in history. That wealth is in the potential of the land and its people. A society's level of poverty is determined by where the wealth of the nation is held and how the people and the land are developed. You can see the wrestle God has with the children of Israel in training them to take responsibility for land. The first generation was unwilling to do this and so they spent 40 years in the desert! In the book of Deuteronomy alone the idea of occupying or taking possession of land appears more than 70 times. The shift in thinking

All nations have wealth. That wealth is in the potential of the land and its people.

is from, "move to the land that will prosper you," to "prosper the land where you are." You must not be scared to contend to own land and with it the consequences of that responsibility. How willing are you to steward land? And more land than you currently have?

NOTES

1.   A discussion of violence and warfare in the Old Testament is more than we have room for in this book, but a sober examination, for example, of Israel's wars with the Canaanites, reveals that God was punishing the Canaanite's wickedness and injustice. God was judging them, and He warned Israel that the same consequences would befall them if they too pursued evil. For a starter to explore this further, visit: www.thegospelcoalition .org/blogs/justin-taylor/how-could-god-command -genocide-in-the-old-testament-2/; accessed March 12, 2024.

2.   One expression of this is what Arthur Burke calls this a nation's "Redemptive Gifts"—see https:// theslg.com/content/the-redemptive-gifts-of-some -nations; accessed March 12, 2024.

6

THE BEAUTY OF YOUR RACE

Like the God in whose image people are made, people are irreducible. There's always more to a person—more stories, more life, more complexities—than we know. The human person, when viewed properly, is unfathomable, incalculable, and dear. Perversion always says otherwise.

—David Dark,
The Sacredness of Questioning Everything

WE ARE FROM ONE BLOOD

Undoubtedly, racial attributes—including skin color, facial features, and height—in nations tell us something new about God.

- When you see white skin or black skin, what does it teach you about the character of God?
- What do your skin color, facial features, and characteristics that are relatively similar within much of your ethnic group, tell of your Creator, as all of His creation reflects His glory?

Let's see what Solomon, the wisest king who ever lived, writes of his beloved:

> *Dark am I, yet lovely, [I am black and beautiful* (NRSV)] *daughters of Jerusalem, dark like the tents of Kedar, like the tent curtains of Solomon* **(Song of Songs 1:5 NIV).**

The Bible links black skin to things that are most exquisite and expensive. Dark equals richness of provision. Dark equals powerful. So when I see a black skin tone, I am supposed to—perhaps subconsciously—be reminded of the powerful, rich provision of God!

> *From one ancestor he made all nations to inhabit the whole earth, and he*

allotted the times of their existence and the boundaries of the places where they would live, so that they would search for God and perhaps grope for him and find him—though indeed he is not far from each one of us. For "In him we live and move and have our being'; as even some of your own poets have said, 'For we too are his offspring'" (Acts 17:26-28 NRSV).

In his wonderful defense of the living, Creator God, Paul makes it implicitly clear that we should not tolerate any sort of racial or national prejudice, because by our physical features we reflect the image of God. He reminds us that from one blood all nations of mankind came—we are single in origin. This should certainly make us question those types of plastic surgery where people try to make themselves look like different races, where we reject looking like the very aspect of God that we were designed to reflect through our body! No race, according to this Scripture, is superior. No nationality should consider itself the cream of humanity, or the best representative of the Kingdom of God.

Tragically, from time to time these concepts have been twisted and somehow made to stand against interracial marriage, but that is not what Paul is saying—in fact he makes quite the opposite point. Cross-racial marriage is a joy, and a sign of how the nations learn of God in their differences. They are a sign of how nations are *supposed* to interact with each other.

No race, according to Acts 17:26-28, is superior. No nationality should consider itself the cream of humanity, or the best representative of the Kingdom of God.

FALLEN CHARACTERISTICS

Apologies to any readers from one of my favorite Greek islands, but, controversially, Paul writes in his letter to Titus that, "*One of Crete's own prophets has said it: 'Cretans are always liars, evil brutes, lazy gluttons.' This saying is true...*" (Titus 1:13 NIV). But here he is identifying the fallen state of a national trait, adopting polemic hyperbole to call an entire population liars and gluttons.

What national trait, in a fallen state, does your nation have? For example, has your nation fallen into greed, or rebellious independence, arrogance, violence, prejudice, superiority, poverty, subservience, or domination?

(Cretans, I think you are a very different people two and a half thousand years on from your poet Epimenides...but your stunning mountain roads do terrify me!)

GLOBALIZATION

There is never any sense in the Bible of us heading toward the goal of becoming one massive, global entity. In fact, Psalm 2 implies that Jesus, the Kingly Son, desires the nations as His heritage—although the poem ends with Him smashing them to pieces, He still wants them presented to Him: *"Ask me, and I will make the nations your inheritance, the ends of the earth your possession"* (Psalm 2:8 NIV).

Jesus's blood has bought people from every ethnic group:

> *And they sang a new song, saying: "You are worthy to take the scroll and to open its seals, because you were slain, and with your blood you purchased for God persons from every*

tribe and language and people and nation" (Revelation 5:9 NIV).

And one day we will worship before Him, a gloriously diverse congregation representing all the people of the earth:

> *After these things I looked, and behold, a great multitude which no one could count, from every nation and all tribes and peoples and tongues, standing before the throne and before the Lamb, clothed in white robes, and palm branches were in their hands; and they cry out with a loud voice, saying, "Salvation to our God who sits on the throne, and to the Lamb"* (Revelation 7:9-10 NASB1995).

We should not have a "globalist agenda" that pursues an empire-like homogeneity (usually Western in form), but there *is* the expectation of learning and cooperating with each other so that Christ is revealed. The nations *together* create a fuller picture of God. He loves diversity—the human family with many distinctives represented, and the total joy of our varied human experiences.

Each nation brings its portion to solve issues that are global in nature.

7

THE DANGER OF EXTREME NATIONALISM

In individuals, insanity is rare; but in groups, parties, nations, and epochs, it is the rule.

—Friedrich Nietzsche,
German Philosopher

Over the last two chapters, our consideration of the value of biblical nationhood and the beauty of race has taken us on a positive journey. However, now we must turn our focus to the unacceptable overdevelopment of a concept of nationhood that is leading much of the church into a form of idolatry that I call "Extreme Nationalism." It is an ultimately deficient worldview that is tempting and enticing for most believers—but is

Warning! Extreme Nationalism is especially dangerous ground for prophets and prophetic people to step onto!

especially dangerous ground for prophets and prophetic people to step onto.

BE WARNED—I WILL PROVOKE YOU

Because of this, and because of how potentially polluting and destructive this issue is (and could further become) to the prophetic movement worldwide, I will pull no punches in this chapter. You *will* read some things that make you feel uncomfortable, and you may be offended by what I write. You will almost certainly be provoked. That is what prophets do, and I make no apologies for this.

All I ask is that you give serious consideration to this issue, and approach it with a humble heart; knowing that this Irish prophet loves you, loves your nation, and loves the church. I love the precious prophetic movement *too much* to stay silent. I could be wrong; but what if I am even a little bit right? What if this Irish prophet is pointing out something that has been hidden in plain sight, obscured by a national blind spot?

> *"Be careful,"* Jesus *warned them. "Watch out for the yeast of the Pharisees and that of Herod"* (Mark 8:15 NIV).

WHAT IS EXTREME NATIONALISM?

"Extreme Nationalism" makes an idol of a state's national identity to the point that its followers will do almost anything to prevent that identity from becoming corrupted by outside influences (especially from foreigners, who are almost always regarded as being in some way inferior).[1]

Some telltale signs of ultranationalism in Europe in the 20th century include:

- Accusing opponents of being "unpatriotic" or even "traitors"
- Extreme attitudes to immigrants, refugees, and border control
- Demonization and dehumanization of political enemies
- Anti-intellectualism, that at its most extreme led to the mistrust of news outlets, universities, and burning of books
- Extreme fear or hatred of different cultures, ethnicities, races, or different religions (with regular fear-mongering rumors about what "they," the enemy within, were getting ready to do to the local population).

- Of course, racism, sexism, misogyny, and a disdain for the weak were also regularly part of this nasty mix.

WHY SHOULD PROPHETS BE CONCERNED?

You might be wondering why we have taken this detour to consider the history and signs of extreme nationalism. Tragically, we Europeans can testify that at nearly any time in our history when extreme nationalism rose up, it was identified in some way with Christianity— and often times was backed by certain wings of the church.[2] Extreme nationalist movements often portray themselves as defenders of Christianity, of "morality" (their version of morality), and of the traditional Christian family—against the perceived rising tide of atheists and the immoral godless masses. In recent years, some "strongmen" leaders in Europe, Asia, and South America have used this message to bolster their cause.

THE DANGER OF EXTREME NATIONALISM TO THE CHURCH

As you read in the previous two chapters, there is absolutely nothing wrong with loving the land that God has birthed or placed you in. We most certainly should be working to see the very best for our nation and our neighbors. There may even be milder aspects of nationalism that are quite compelling, such as the emphasis on conservative family values and a leaning toward some aspects of traditional Judeo-Christian morality.

However, if we allow nationalist and political ideologies to become the driver and motivation for growing our churches and changing our nation, then we can potentially fall into a trap of extreme *Christian* nationalism. This is what happened in Great Britain during its colonial era and throughout the century of the Victorian Empire—and has also emerged in the United States in recent decades. It is definitely not unique to the USA, but because the church is still (relatively) large and strong in North America, extreme nationalism is currently fueling fires of division and has the potential to drive many away from Jesus, rather than into His arms.

Extreme nationalism perpetuates the notion that the United States of America was founded as a Christian country and therefore we believers must fight tooth and nail to recover this utopia, across every inch of society. Sociologists Andrew Whitehead and Samuel Perry describe this ideology as, "the belief that America has been and always should be distinctively Christian from top to bottom, in its self-identity, interpretations of its own history, sacred symbols, cherished values, and public policies, and it aims to keep it this way."[3] As an eventual consequence of this narrative, proponents of this extremist ideology would argue that we should not strictly divide between church and state; they imply that it is only evil secularists who want to separate them.

Extreme nationalism in the USA has its goal to reclaim the glory of America (note, not God), and to do this—to make America amazing again—you must Christianize all politics.

You and I might find ourselves nodding in agreement with some of its slogans, such as:

- The nation is weakened by taking God out of politics.
- Society is deformed by secularism.
- Darwinian and Marxist theories have helped undermine the fabric and morality of the nation.

- Only by putting a Christian party in power can the nation be returned to conservative family values and morals.
- The church is useful as a political lobbying power.

But these ideas have further grown into Christian tribalism between the two parties—Republican versus Democrat, where one party's victory is considered akin to national salvation, but the other alternative is hell on earth. It is nothing short of the politicization of faith, where people outwork their faith majoritively in the political arena.

- Under this extreme nationalism, faith doesn't stand outside of politics but rather faith and politics become one and the same.
- The church becomes secondary to the role of government and the justice system in the land because only they are perceived to have the power to legislate and pass laws that will enforce the morality that nation needs.
- Extreme nationalism also believes the statement that, "My nation has an extra special place in God's heart, and therefore

we are the standard of nationhood to attain to."

So far, so good, you might think when you read this. But beware, the goal of this form of extreme nationalism, sometimes called Christian nationalism, is not about true Christianity. Instead, Christianity is used as a pawn (just as the nationalist parties in 20th century Europe did) to achieve their real goal, which is to get what *they* want—their own political and cultural dominance. When you listen to them, extreme nationalists never talk about life and relationship with God, only about all the blessings that they expect to get from God for themselves and their country, be that the USA or elsewhere.

At its core, this false ideology is about earthly good, worldly blessings, national success and power, the blessings of God for our own country above all others—and even at the expense of all others. Success, money, health, and fame! Jesus is just the means to access all this and obtain a stronger, more powerful, more successful country. But if Jesus ever becomes just the means to an end and not the goal, that's idolatry. Rather than making our nations more Christian, this false ideology of extreme nationalism does the opposite, taking us all further away from the true message of the Kingdom.

Prophets must not allow themselves to become caught up in the patriotic fervor of extreme nationalism. There are times when its ideologies might sound like they are straight from Scripture but beware, a great deception is afoot, one that satan has used time and time again throughout history, across continents.

LOSING SIGHT OF THE KINGDOM

Under the influence of extreme nationalism, the church becomes secondary to the role of government in the land because only it has the power to legislate and pass laws that will enforce the morality that nation needs.

It seems that as believers become more politically engaged, they often become less *theologically* engaged because of the sweeping, all-consuming need to defend a party or political ideology. This leads to myopic, "micro-level" behavior—backing a single political party, exalting a single leader, putting one's hope in a single term of office. (This is in opposition to seeing things through

As believers become more politically engaged, they become less theologically engaged because of the need to defend their political ideology.

the "macro-level" arc of biblical hermeneutics.[4]) In doing so, we lose sight of the overall story of God, the crucial message of His Kingdom, and we even become blind to basic biblical doctrines and foundations. We want our political party to rule and reign rather than the Kingdom. Or we believe that the only way the Kingdom can come in is via the party gaining victory and controlling government.

WE'VE BEEN HERE BEFORE

British missionaries in the 18th and 19th centuries set about not just sharing the good news but also Westernizing every place they went to, expanding the Empire. They were the original "extreme Christian nationalists" in essence,[5] and many of them went beyond basic evangelism that simply states that "Our Savior God is all you need," and strayed into, "Our government, systems, and our politics is what you need."

AUGUSTINE'S TWO CITIES

From as far back as biblical times, kings and queens have often sought to rule by "divine right"—in other words, their right to rule is given by God and only God can judge them; these monarchs are not accountable to any earthly authority. This continued until as recently as Henry VIII in England, Louis XIV in France, and King James VI in Scotland (as in the "King James Bible"). In extreme cases, the bishops of the church answer to the monarch. On the other hand, Catholic doctrine taught that the pope has ultimate authority over the Church, and therefore indirectly over the state—many popes exercised authority over European states down through the centuries.

Perhaps the most influential theologian on this topic was Augustine of Hippo (354-430) who believed that there should be an overlap between the "earthly, temporal city" (the state) and the "city of God" (the church). Rather than separating church and state, Augustine proposed the view that it was the work of the "temporal city" to facilitate the establishing of a "heavenly city" on earth. So, for almost a millennium and a half, the world and the church occupied a tightly bound relationship, as kings used the church, and the church used kings.

MARRYING CHURCH AND STATE

At its core, extreme nationalism does not just use the church and the name of Christ in order to gain political influence and power. When it infects Christianity, it deceives the church into an arranged *marriage* with the political system. It builds on the writings and practice of theologians such as Augustine, Calvin, and their proteges, whose ideologies washed generations with a single invention that dominates us today—you (the church) must use the state as a means to put down heresy; you must do whatever it costs to get the political system to back the church's truth.[6]

> **Christian nationalism teaches that you must use the state as a means to put down heresy.**

The thought that underpins this lie is that *nations change because politics change.* This is a fundamental misunderstanding of the entire gospel and how the Kingdom of God functions. Extreme nationalism in the church wants political clout rather than being salt and light, the yeast, the wheat-among-the-tares, which are the very things that restrict unrighteousness in the community.

The central lie that the church needs the state for survival swaps the power of God for the glory that satan offers through the systems of the world. What Jesus rejected at His temptation we have fully embraced.

> *The devil led him up to a high place and showed him in an instant all the kingdoms of the world. And he said to him, "I will give you all their authority and splendor; it has been given to me, and I can give it to anyone I want to. If you worship me, it will all be yours"* (Luke 4:5-7 NIV).

The church should not look to the world to come to its aid. The *ecclesia* should have no need to look to man-made structures and

The fundamental misunderstanding is that nations change because politics change.

The massive, underpinning thought that we gain from the Anabaptists is that the church and the state are two different, separate kingdoms. systems to rescue it, fund it, defend it, or legislate for it. The church only looks to politics to put down heresy and back its stance because it has lost its understanding of the power of God and how the Kingdom of Christ works! Therefore, we can confidently assert that the understanding of the power and the Kingdom of God must have been lost for multiple generations, which has left the church little option but to partner with a wrong, empire-orientated power—a partnership that married it to politics.

THE ANABAPTISTS

On one side we have Protestant reformers including Martin Luther, Jean Calvin, and John Knox, who utilized the authority of the state to put down heresy, as Augustine had suggested a thousand years earlier. On the other hand, we have the theological traditions that come from the Anabaptists. (Anabaptist means re-baptized.)

The Anabaptists wanted separate leaders in the church and the state because they understood that the church and the state were two different kingdoms and could not be allowed to mix. Theirs was a strong doctrine of a godly, separated remnant, and this still influences some today. This godly, separate remnant believe that nations are good (see the Biblical Nationhood chapter), but that they have boundaries and an end as directed by God, and our hope is not in a political order.

We must not be a church in withdrawal but instead must be a purified and powerful influence, captivating people with Jesus and making citizens of the Kingdom of God. I believe, similarly to the Anabaptists, that the Kingdom of God and the state need to be clearly separated so that you can choose which Kingdom you are with. The leaven of Herod must not be allowed to pollute the Kingdom of God!

SEPARATING CHURCH AND STATE

When Martin Luther kickstarted the Protestant Reformation, he began to seed the ideas of "two kingdoms," the beginnings of separation of church and state. From the 1500s, we began to see three camps emerge. On one extreme, the Roman Catholic and Anglican Church have retained a deeply interwoven relationship between church and state. In many nations Catholicism is the state religion and the Church of England (Anglican) is so entwined that the British King occupies the role of "Defender of the Faith" and its bishops sit in the upper legislative chamber.

In the middle, Presbyterian reformers such as Luther, Calvin, and Knox recognized the two kingdoms and the need to be freer from state-interference, stressing the saving faith required by each of us as individuals. Despite their theology, they could never quite break free from influence of political government, championing what they saw as the God-ordained role of the state to promote good and punish evil. They saw the power of using the state to put down heresy and stamp out sin via law and legislation. In some senses, this ideology has viewed governments and politicians as tools of the church, a means by which to dominate national culture to their religious ends. This is why you find, in parts of Calvinistic Scotland, official council signs forbidding children from entering playgrounds on Sundays!

Finally, the most radical of reformers in the 1500s, the Anabaptists, agreed with Luther about two kingdoms but went much further, arguing for a complete separation and creating rules that banned believers from voting, serving in public office, or participating in any other way with the "kingdom of the world."

Eventually English philosopher John Locke, perhaps the most influential political thinker when it came to Thomas Jefferson and the USA's founders, came up with a workable, practical theory for how a nation could be run with a complete separation of church and state (even so, Locke believed that atheism should be outlawed!). In practice, the phrase "separation of church and state" never actually made it into the Constitution and twelve of the first thirteen states were free to appoint official religions.

THE FALSE SAVIOR OF NATIONALISM

Every ideology has a savior, with an end time goal, or aim. To the Scottish, William Wallace, the outlaw of Braveheart, was the savior, and the end goal was an independent, free Scotland. To the extreme nationalist, political, righteous leaders are the saviors, and the end goal is a great nation with God's righteous laws at its heart. In this you can guarantee that one day you will be disappointed, because nations rise and fall (Job 12:23). In biblical theology, Jesus is the Savior, and the end-time goal is His return and the ultimate fullness of His Kingdom, Heaven and earth reunited.

To the extreme Christian nationalist, political, righteous leaders are the saviors, and the end goal is a great nation with God's righteous laws at its heart.

The New Testament never teaches us to think in terms of the salvation of territory; but instead to think of an individual who comes into the Kingdom. Salvation is only possible through an individual door where, on repentant confession of your sin and acknowledging Jesus Christ as Lord, you receive eternal life and citizenship of the Kingdom.[7] The Kingdom of God is advanced by personal relationship and increases, one individual at a time. It is a faith focused on the changing of hearts.

In other words, you don't automatically inherit it from your parents, or achieve entrance to it because of the nation or the state that you live in, nor by the nature of the laws of the land. It is only and ever possessed one at a time, by individual belief. After all, no one decided on *your* behalf that you were going to be a Christian, did they?

This means we cannot talk about "national salvation."

ARE THERE SHEEP AND GOAT NATIONS?

There is no concept of "sheep nations" and "goat nations" in the Bible. If you've ever heard teaching that there is, it has come from a poor translation of Matthew 25 verse 32, which says:

The New Testament never teaches us to think in terms of the salvation of territory but instead of individuals who come, one by one, into the Kingdom.

*All the nations will be gathered before Him, and He will separate **the people** one from another as a shepherd separates the sheep from the goats* (Matthew 25:32 NIV).

Jesus is telling us that the people get separated, not the nations. We will all be gathered as the countries of the world before Him, as He is seated on His throne, and then individuals will be divided, one from another. Up to this point in the future, people will have lived together as wheat and tares in nations. Now they are brought before the judgment throne and separated according to the faith decision made by *each individual*. The judging process of God is not looking at the righteousness of the land or the territory (that's a Muslim thought!). God judges the heart of every individual person in His creation.

Can a political party structure accept Jesus as its Savior? Is the land ever made righteous because of the quality of a law? What has the law ever saved? The misteaching of the concept of sheep and goat nations drives us into a form of Christian nationalism where we work for the power of politics, rather than the (spiritual) power of the church. The concept of a "Christian nation"—or a "non-Christian nation" for that matter—is biblical nonsense. A country can't acquire or reject salvation, only individual people can!

No nation can be founded as a "Christian nation"; it is simply not possible. Certainly, a state can be established on Christian *values*, godly *justice*, and biblically based *law*, but this makes the nation moral, not saved. It may give it a set of good principles but that does not guarantee any heart change in its citizens. You can have founding principles that aid a nation toward adopting Judeo-Christian behavioral tendencies (and I celebrate this), but this will never make you righteous before God. God looks at an individual's heart, not at your structure or constitution.

If the idea that Matthew 25:32 refers to people and not nations is new to you, please see the Appendix at the back of this book, which goes into more detail on this passage and shows how the erroneous teaching came into the church.

The judging process of God is not looking at the righteousness of the land or the territory (that's a Muslim thought!). God judges the heart of every individual person in His creation.

Of course, there are Christian politicians whom we desperately want to back, pray for, and encourage. And, on the days when the options don't present themselves as clearly as godly versus ungodly candidates to choose from at the polling booth (as is frequently the case in Britain), well, perhaps the outcome isn't as important as we think it is. After all, the gospel is a gospel of salvation and Kingdom, not the gospel of political change. As stated earlier, the Kingdom of God is revolutionary and dangerous to all other powers!

No modern geopolitical nation state is "one nation under God." Within each nation on earth are members of God's Kingdom who are a chosen people; and, as the apostle writes in 1 Peter 2:9, they are *"a royal priesthood"* and *"God's special possession."* They are His *"holy nation"* (Kingdom) by virtue of being called *"from darkness into His wonderful light."* Peter goes on to amplify this thought in the following verses, so that we understand that those who have taken up the citizenship of the Kingdom of God are living godly lives in the midst of pagan societies, *"as foreigners and exiles,"* strangers in this world—they are in the world, but not of it.

TO WHICH KINGDOM ARE YOU AVAILABLE?

The Kingdom of God is available to you in the here and the now. But the real question is whether you are available to the Kingdom? The Kingdom of God is not in partnership with other kingdoms, nor does it rely on other kingdoms. It is not an equal to other kingdoms. The church does not go about the business of another kingdom.

Many of the parables in Scripture about the Kingdom of God show that the Kingdom grows in an almost imperceptible way: it is *wheat among the tares*; it is *yeast in dough*; it is revolutionary subterfuge that is not always recognizable. The Kingdom is present, and it is infectious! We must do better in distrusting the kingdoms of this world and we must uncouple from the lie that politics saves a nation.

> **We must uncouple from the lie that politics saves a nation.**

CAN A NATION BE COVENANTED?

We often think that we can covenant our nations to God, but this is not a biblical reality and is not backed up by history. In 1638, Scotland attempted to make a "Solemn League and Covenant" to be covenanted to God. Promises were made by every Scottish church leader in the churchyard of Grey-friars Kirk in Edinburgh. The Covenant was sent the length and breadth of the nation, to every town and village, and was signed by huge numbers of the population. If you could not write your name, you signed in your own blood. Following this, during what the Scottish church called the "golden decade," or "The Rule of the Saints," it began to dawn on the people that they were no longer free and were instead under the grip of a merciless religious theocracy. One of its leaders gleefully remarked that:

> Scotland is in her flower. There is no family so obscure that [the Church] cannot probe its sinfulness. No scandalous person can live, no scandal can be concealed in all Scotland because of the strict correspondence between ministers and congregation. The only

complaint of profane people is this: they have no liberty to sin.[8]

Scotland soon became a world where children were prosecuted and jailed for failing to honor their parents; where executions were a daily occurrence; men, women, and children flogged, nailed by their ears to post, holes bored in their tongues. The covenanted people were knee-deep in their neighbors' blood and guts. Soon the violence extended into civil war, religious terrorism, and the execution of a king. Scotland had become a law-based state, and its leaders were power-hungry dictators flying a church flag—within ten years it had all fallen apart.

Biblically, only God makes covenants with nations, not the other way around. This is something He chooses to do, and in the entirety of scripture He only made it with one people group. Soberly, after the Tower of Babel incident, God disinherited the nations, keeping a covenant relationship with Israel, a people who He called his own.

When the Most High apportioned the nations, at his dividing up of the sons of humankind, he fixed the boundaries of the peoples, according to the number of the children of Israel. For Yahweh's portion was his people, Jacob the share of his inheritance (**Deuteronomy 32:8-9 Lexham English Bible**).

Though the Scots were full of good intentions, they failed to keep their Covenant, because it is not feasible to keep one that we initiate. In our sin we will always break the terms. Paul unpacks in Romans that the old covenant (God promises to bless His people if they listen to Him and keep His laws—Exodus 19:5-8) was never going to be successful. Its terms were impossible to keep because humans always fall short (Romans 3:23).

Only God makes covenants with nations, not the other way around.

Jesus is not interested in you or I marrying our land or even Him marrying our land; or our covenanting territory to Him. He wants to marry His bride *only* and will exclusively make eternal vows with her. The future of covenant is one that is written on our hearts, not in statute books, constitutions, or in the words and decrees of well-meaning intercessors.

"This is the covenant I will make with the people of Israel after that time," declares the Lord. *"I will put my law in their minds and write it on their hearts. I will be their God, and they will be my people"* **(Jeremiah 31:33 NIV).**

In Old Testament Israel, it was through the act of circumcision that you gave the sign that you had become a member of the "nation." Now in the New Testament, it is believers' baptism that is the sign that brings you into membership of the Kingdom. The new, unbreakable covenant was made between Father and Son at the Cross. Jesus bought us into this by His blood, and so the only covenant we are now looking forward to is on the day when we, the members of the Kingdom, the bride, are joined to the Bridegroom at the wedding feast of the Lamb!

NOTES

1. (The fascists, who we considered briefly in Chapter 2, were big on extreme nationalism, also known as ultranationalism.) Historically, extreme nationalism has been a problem in Europe, especially in the 20th century (for example in Germany, Italy, Spain) but still regularly rears its head in the 21st, especially in Eastern Europe and Russia. There are forms of extreme nationalism rising in other continents too—in India, some South American countries, and even North America.

2. According to Britannica, movements were found in Poland, Spain, Portugal, France, Austria, Hungary, Croatia, Bolivia, Argentina, Chile, Brazil, Romania, France, and Spain. Fascists in German and Italy also posed as protectors of the church but their ideologies contained many elements that conflicted with traditional Christian beliefs and their policies were sometimes opposed by church leaders.

3. Andrew Whitehead and Samuel Perry, *Taking America Back for God: Christian Nationalism in the United States* (London: Oxford University Press, 2020).

4. Hermeneutics deals with studying how best to interpret the biblical. By "macro-level arc" I mean

looking at the whole arc of Scripture, from Genesis to Revelation.

5.   Even before this, John Knox and his reformers in Scotland had Christian nationalist tendencies by ordaining Presbyterianism as a state religion and going as far as establishing a theocratic form of government.

6.   To be fair, the church was doing this long before the Protestant Reformation—during the Spanish Inquisition, for example. These problems began with (Roman Emperor) Constantine, if not before.

7.   Marked by the sacrament of baptism, of course.

8.   From *A History of Scotland* by Neil Oliver (Phoenix, AZ: Phoenix Publisher, 2011).

8

PATRIOTISM VERSUS EXTREME NATIONALISM

But seek first the kingdom of God
and His righteousness, and all these
things shall be added to you.

—Matthew 6:33 NKJV

THE PRIDE OF A NATION

It is a requirement that you love your nation, pray for your nation, and impact your nation. But when you forget that the Kingdom of God is higher, is preeminent, and is to be chased and apprehended above all, and that God is sovereign, you misplace how you see your nation in the overall hierarchy of the universe, resulting in ever-increasing extremes of nationalism. Extreme nationalism is patriotism gone wrong.

How much time do you spend thinking about your nation versus how much time do you spend asking how you can extend the Kingdom of God? We may have a passport that is proof of our earthly nationality, but we can place too much emphasis on our citizenship of that nation and not enough emphasis on being part of the international family of God.

This idolatry starts with loving our neighbor, serving our city, adoring our nation, and being a good patriot, but then nationalism grows out of misplaced patriotism. The quest, therefore, is to rightly prioritize, and to develop in us a *small* idea of patriotism that is present but not dominant. We need a little idea of patriotism.

Nationalism is patriotism gone wrong. Nationalism grows out of misplaced patriotism.

The nation must not become divine in our thinking. Unhinged patriotism leads to a mindset where the nation becomes *as God* or becomes the standard by which all other nations fall short. Where there is the pride of superiority in the hearts of a people, the Lord is forced to resist them. How would you score the pride level in your own nation?

How many nations have inadvertently fallen into the trap of believing that they are the model of knowledge, the standard of how education must be applied, the pinnacle of wisdom, the benchmark of progress, the gold standard of an economic system, and the absolute example of the right form of government? This screams to every onlooker that, "you need to become like us, for we have attained greatness and therefore are *the* authority," it speaks a haughty rhetoric, which then becomes the language of conflict. Once we become smug and pompous, we lose the humility of peace-making, diplomacy, negotiation, and serving. Rich and powerful nations have displayed a history of thinking that they have a divine right, a *manifest destiny*, to shape the future according to their own agenda.

TRIBALISM—NATIONALISM WITHIN BORDERS

Beyond nation against nation, when extreme nationalism is within your own borders, the demonic spirit will continue its agenda to silo people away into defensive and insular tribes, where each faction believes that it has the monopoly on truth and it becomes the seedbed for civil wars.

The subtle side of this has begun to take a foothold on our social media platforms, where we feel more affinity with our dog walking club, sports club, conspiracy theory club, or political club than we do with the nation.

UNTEACHABLE NATIONALISM

The concern for believers amid days when God is shaking mankind, should be that we avoid retreating back to unteachable nationalism, where we hunker down and defend our nation as being perfect and the answer to everything. However, you don't prevent the extremes of nationalism by coercing nations to become members of homogenous entities like, for example the European Union (EU), or other international alliances. After all, we are not cookie-cutter nations. Instead, it must press us into the place of teaching biblical nationhood; in other words, teach the God-given value of each nation but also the supreme, rescuing power of the Kingdom of Heaven.

GROWING UNDER PERSECUTION

Since we have built our thinking around Jesus's Kingdom being revolutionary and dangerous to all other powers, we must consider how ill-received our radical, subversive rhetoric will be within the boundaries of our nations. The gospel is going to be offensive to rulers and their systems, and it is going to get us persecuted.

Nearly all of Jesus's disciples were painfully martyred: crucified upside down, boiled in oil, and beheaded. They suffered greatly for their faith and met with these violent deaths because of their bold witness. I have often found it challenging to read Hebrews 11 without tears in my eyes as the faithful's journeys into martyrdom are described: being sawn in two, stoned, mistreated, destitute and persecuted (Hebrews 11:3). Living in deserts, caves, and holes in the ground, these mighty men and women were commended for their faith. None of this came to them because they spoke *only* of the love of God.

The persecuted church today is not chased down by governments because of their sweet worship. No! The disciples and the persecuted were, and continue to be, a real threat to the *status quo* of the nation. The Kingdom of King Jesus is dangerous to all man-made and satanically inspired kingdoms of this world.

Painfully, we must come to acknowledge that the church is at its best under persecution. But when it is pandered to and given space within a nation, it becomes fat, irrelevant, impotent, and powerless. Without exception, the church grows virulently in extreme opposition. Satan knows that the best thing he can do is have the state bless the people of God.

Without exception, the church grows virulently in extreme opposition. Satan knows that the best thing he can do is have the state bless the people of God.

In the early church, the Christians were not waving the Roman flag! Rome was so hostile to the people of God that they would have no part in elevating Rome as a champion nation. The Greek word for *witness*, became the English word for *martyr*. To testify for Jesus cost you your life.

Are your first thoughts as a prophetic person:

- "How do I protect, guard, and shore up my nation?"

- "How do I get politics to bless the church more?"

Or do you ask more Kingdom-orientated questions:

- "Father, where is my nation in the arc of its history, and what do You want to do with it right now?"
- "How far have the people in my nation fallen from giving You any place, Lord?"
- "How could I speak the Kingdom more to them?"

STOP PROTECTING BABYLON

Protecting our nation has become a religion. Today, if you realized you lived in Babylon (a nation hostile to God), would you pray, "God bless Babylon?" or, "God I want Babylon to increase?" Or would you wave a Babylonian flag?

Or would you instead pray Kingdom prayers such as, "God, bless the remnant to rise and be strengthened, so that they may be a radical signpost for Jesus Christ!"? Surely we know that we don't pray to bless the kingdoms of this world.

Surely we know that we don't mark our bodies or wave the flags of the kingdoms of this world?

In a moment of unadulterated honesty, let us ask the question, "Is my nation like Babylon?" For if it is, it is likely that God will be in pruning mode—shaking and course correcting. We must be open to rethink what we are, and ask, "In light of where we are, is my nation on a trajectory for judgment or for blessing, for mercy or for consequences, for exile or for freedom?" Prophets, please let's be vigilant in how we pray for our nations! Let us ask for the gift of the discerning of spirits, that we might know with which spirit we are interceding and prophesying over them.

We are strangers in exile, a diaspora waiting for our coming King. We pray for the nation, but we want to get back "home." Our nations are of *this* world and Christians must live in every country of the world as those who are just passing through. Watch how you think through symbols like flags, the saluting of flags, the raising of flags—how you do it and *why* you do it can easily get mangled in your heart. With what spirit do you sing a national anthem or read a constitution?

We are never taught by Jesus to pray, "God bless our nation." Rather, we are taught to pray instead that *His Kingdom would come.* We should begin by praying for our fellow Kingdom of God members across the nation, that they would be bold to demonstrate the liberating power of Jesus. When we pray for His Kingdom to come, we are, in essence, expecting that the kingdoms of this world—and their glory and comfort—will be shaken, not supported.

UNTEACHABLE NATIONALISM, EMPIRE SPIRIT

Down the slippery slope we go! Minds close, hearts are hardened, patriotism has become nationalism, and extreme nationalism in turn has become an empire spirit. In this place the demons are speaking, and they have a Christian audience!

When locked in empire spirit or unteachable nationalism, learning from anyone else who is not an echo chamber of our own thoughts is out of the question. We will only accept what reflects hard and half "truths" to us. Here is where racism breeds until it becomes a dominant part of culture. All forms of suspicion abound, as siloed groups create common enemies of everyone bearing any difference who might sharpen them. Xenophobia is the norm. Conspiracy theories that further bolster assumptions run rampant.

Ultimately this extreme partnership with a demon of empire creates a deep fear of being overrun, or a fear of losing what you have. It is worked out through a domination mindset, where the subjugation of many seems reasonable, therefore another's poverty, lack of education, or pain is easy to overlook and justify. It is fear-fueled and also creates fear in its subjects. This mindset says, after all, "We don't want anyone rising to rob us." We can speak of their equity, but we will not empower it.

When we pray for Jesus's Kingdom to come, we expect that the kingdoms of this world—and their glory and comfort—will be shaken, not supported.

"In God we trust" becomes "in *our* might we trust." Leaning on the everlasting arms of the Savior becomes leaning on my man-made boundaries and being able to stand against anyone who on the surface looks different. It becomes about protecting and defending for yourself. It believes in the right to be weaponized against another. Occasionally it has the face of *enforcing* morality or truth, enforcing righteousness because you want others to be saved. However, as we saw in the example of Scotland's "Rule of the Saints" period, domination and subjugation will never bear truly righteous fruit—when the root is rotten, the tree cannot bear good fruit (Matthew 12:33).

Empires set themselves up to be a rival to Jesus Christ because, to them, their version of truth *is* the truth. Empires are ultimately about self-deification. When this overtakes a land, the subjugated tend to, in time, eventually arise with a militant desire to overthrow. However, it is noteworthy that often the rise of the subjugated is fueled by their own unresolved trauma and pain, and they in turn step into cycles of domination, retribution, and retaliation, and repeat the patterns of history—if they are not squashed violently first.

Empire spirit sees the superiority complex fully matured, with anger and fear pulsating close to the surface. God hates the arrogance of empire manifested in those who feel they have nothing to learn. In this place we have become the "Unteachable Church" with a doctrine of unteachable nationalism.

When this sweeps into the House of God we begin playing our own version of church, building defensive walls up against aspects of truth that others hold. The demonic spirit now guides churches under its power into heresy hunting, with robust inquisition-like task forces set up (under the misapplied guise of Matthew 18) to narrow the door of acceptable behavior.

When empire is in crisis and feels its grip loosening, it over-polices its boundaries because it fears decline, thus leading to a church that does unintended damage. We may also call this "territorial spirits" or "oligarchy," where rule is in the hands of a few with religious control. The people of God become pharisaical (like the Pharisees), overplaying their hand in crisis, and diminishing. The church becomes extremely divided with "be suspicious" as a mantra. Intimacy is now almost impossible because vulnerability is undermined, and it is unsafe to display your heart. Your only option for survival is to become numb but in numbness all tenderness to the Spirit of God is lost, leading to a spiritually impotent and sterile people.

God hates the arrogance of empire manifested in those who feel they have nothing to learn.

UNTEACHABLE AND PROTECTIONIST

At this point we tend to hear the loud voice of the deconstructionists who want *all* things in current

---

church structures to be decimated, burnt to the ground! This idea while perhaps having some merit, only reinforces the oligarchs' need to protect what they have. (Although I am painting a picture of the most extreme form of empire within the church, I'm sure that we can identify some version of this within Western Christendom.) An example of this protectionism is found in the ancestors of the Protestant Reformation.

As I described in the Introduction, I grew up within a Protestant culture, one that predominantly displayed "Unteachable Protestantism" at its core. It was highly skilled in the art of disagreement and division! Protestantism, with its one billion adherents, must now know that, despite the glory it brought to many, its shadowy side trained our deep, emotional default setting into being able to say, "We are not one church, and we are not one family." It justified the notion that we don't ever need to change—just keep splitting— was acceptable. The irony is that we have inherited from the so-called Reformation the deeply held thought of "separate rather than reform" (though you'll rarely hear this expressed out loud).

Unteachable Protestantism deeply connects to empire and feels pride in declaring, "I won't be sharpened by you; I won't learn from you—you have nothing to teach me that is worthwhile". This is the church in mature un-teach-ability and is frequently associated with unteachable nationalism.

Protestantism makes the notion that we don't ever need to reform acceptable.

The church is always the government of God on earth. Our job is to shadow atmospheres and so, when we the church are unteachable, defensive, aggressive, and territorial, we shadow nations and they have become as defensive as us. When the church makes enemies of other churches it leads to nations making enemies of other nations. In the days of war, are we brave enough to ask if *we* have sown the seeds of war, because church-against-church presets the condition for nation-against-nation? What we model the nation will become!

HUMILITY AND SUBMISSION

God, in His mercy and unrelenting kindness, steps in to break us. There is only one solution if we find ourselves in this place of defensive division, and that is the deep, lamenting cry for humility and submission to Jesus Christ. Rather than fight for

Yield to the Spirit of God, that we might become carriers of His fullness, rather than full of ourselves. our own elevation and dominance, that we would yield ourselves to the Spirit of God, where His Spirit would fill our spirit, where our flesh would be dominated by Him, so that we might become carriers of His fullness, rather than full of ourselves.

If we are offended and triggered all of the time, we are living in the extension of the flesh and under the influence the kingdoms of this world. You can never extend the Kingdom of Heaven if you stay in this place.

PRAYER

Father, forgive me. I am sorry for how I so easily slid into defensiveness and protectionism. Lord, where there is a spirit of division, and separation I repent, and I break agreement with these ideas now.

If I allowed my patriotism to become something darker, I am sorry, Lord. I confess of every time when I have, knowingly or unknowingly, become idolatrous in how I saw my nation, or other nations, and where I put my hope, trust, and allegiance toward it, rather than You. I choose to seek first Your Kingdom!

Having repented and broken agreement with these things, I now reject every demonic spirit of pride, nationalism, and tribalism that has oppressed me. I tell them, "Get out of me now, in the name of Jesus Christ. You may no longer have influence over me."

I declare the truth that I am a child of Christ, adopted into a new family, a royal priesthood. I am first and foremost a citizen of His Kingdom, not the nation I feel patriotic about.

Holy Spirit, would You fill me afresh with the zeal of the Lord, that I would love Your ways above the ways of the world? Give me courage, that I may not fear this temporal existence, nor the necessary shakings, for I know that my eternal destiny is a New Heaven and a New Earth. Amen.

9

GOD AND POLITICS

I am quite sure now that often, very
often, in matters concerning religion
and politics a man's reasoning powers
are not above the monkeys.

—Mark Twain

What was your childhood dream? Secretly, I
always wanted to be Prime Minister of the United
Kingdom! In my first week of studying Politics at
university, at the impressionable age of 18, I joined
a political party and put highly opinionated, party-political posters on the wall of my dorm room.
Personally incensed at the change to the pay-
ment methods for university fees, to say I felt let
down by the existing political system would have
been an understatement!

However, as I studied, disillusion followed as
doubts and questions over what politics could
actually achieve swept over me. Shifting to major
in Sociology, I spent many hours profiling serial
killers in an attempt to understand what happens

to those in society when they go mad. Along with this I trained as a counselor in a pro-life charity—in case that was how one could really transform society.

It is the power of God working through the people of God who bring true transformation.

Eventually, aged 22, a graduate, and newly married, I decided that business was how the world is changed, so I retrained. It took me on a circuitous and undulating journey to understand that, in fact, it is the power of God working through the people of God who bring true transformation.

Somewhere along the way my husband, David, and I, had finally allowed Matthew 16 to get under our skin, where the government of God is *only* put on the church, nowhere else. Nothing else is as blessed by God with His transformative power, and His rulership capabilities, as the *ecclesia,* His people.

> ...*and on this rock I will build my* [ecclesia], *and the gates of Hades will not overcome it* (Matthew 16:18 NIV).

Now, after 25 years of marriage, we are captivated more than ever by the need for transformation, and the questions of *how* the power of God is best displayed in the nations, through the church, still form the core of many dinner table chats.

WHAT IS THE BIBLE'S POLITICAL PHILOSOPHY?

Perhaps you will have read the errors of Christian nationalism at its extremes and the empire spirit in the previous chapters and wondered if they're really all that bad! As we venture deeper together to see, we will examine what God really says about politics. Let me begin by asking you some questions:

- How politically motivated and orientated are you?
- Do you have strong political party affiliations or memberships?
- Do you love politics?
- *Should* you love politics?

How you answer these questions is rooted in what you think success is.

WHAT DOES SUCCESS LOOK LIKE?

Overall, most of us believe that success is a big church, a Christian in political office, the ability to gather in a way of our choosing, church buildings owned, Christian laws, a dominant voice in politics, and a landscape where the church is the cornerstone of our modern, Western communities, and where the people of God are accepted by society.

We think about having influence, thus *having significant influence* is a fundamental motivator to us. We value popularity as a sense of arriving and achieving. The size of our "audience" has become a crucial measurement for us; therefore, we value breadth rather than depth. We prefer high-visibility, top-down domination in our cities, states, and nations, with compromise necessary to remain in place. We celebrate contemporary appeal, where true discipleship is *implied* rather than actioned.

But what if success is none of these things?

What if success is a church thriving under rejection, beautifully intolerant to society's values? What if success is small rooms and high-risk decisions that seek to liberate rather than dominate.

Surely a *holy* appeal rather than a *contemporary* appeal is more desirable.

WHAT DOES RIGHTEOUSNESS IN A NATION LOOK LIKE?

> *Righteousness exalts a nation* (Proverbs 14:34 NIV).

It is not that having Christians in influence exalts a nation, or that key election results exalt a nation, but rather that *righteousness* brings a nation before God. How would we go about measuring this?

What if success is a church thriving under rejection, holy and beautifully intolerant to society's values, valuing high-risk liberation rather than compromised domination?

What is a biblical measurement of a righteous nation? What is your measurement—or perceived destination or arrival point—for your nation to be considered righteous? Of course we want righteous laws, but would these make us a righteous nation? The answer is, "No." After all, there are a number of ultra-conservative nations in the world (usually Muslim dominant) where no abortion is allowed, no pornography is permitted, no homosexuality is tolerated, and so on. Are these "righteous" nations? No!

Fundamentally, Christianity begins with, and is measured by, the condition of people's hearts. Your access to the Kingdom of Heaven has never been granted on the basis of your law-keeping, nor your rule-setting, or law-making. The law *never* saved anyone. Certainly, law-keeping is a reasonable measurement of a wholesome society, but it is not the biblical route to salvation.

Do I want abortion banned? Yes. For years I labored as a media spokesperson for the pro-life lobby, working on television and radio, putting forward the anti-abortion case. Nevertheless, if I secured an anti-abortion law, would it make my nation more righteous before God? Absolutely not!

Islam and the Christianity are opposite in how they think regarding stewarding societies. True Christianity is motivated by starting with the heart and personal transformation because of an individual belief in the lordship of Jesus Christ. When Jesus has your heart, He also has all you own, all you are, how you vote, and how you manage your money, because you willingly lay it down at His feet.

On the other hand, Islam begins with law, behavior, and territory. One of its core values must be that of an enforced takeover of all of society. A top-down setting of the cultural tone, achieved through law changes (that *everyone* must abide by), is inevitably regarded as a necessary and desirable result. This oppressively enforces a code of morality through submission to the ruling religious power. No one chooses—it is dictated and set by what the leaders perceive to be righteous laws that they believe will bring Islam's version of "salvation" to the nation.

Christianity works in reverse to Islam's top-down religious control. Because every person responds to Christ's invitation individually, it is never about a law being thrust upon them; it is a personal heart change. From that response they, guided by the Spirit of Jesus, *choose* biblical morality. For example, this means that when we're talking about abortion, any anti-abortion law would become obsolete through no one needing it.

Your access to Heaven has never been granted on your law-keeping or law-making. The law never saved anyone.

Through faith in Jesus, not through legislation, a wave of individuals will choose to reject the murder of innocents and pursue life. Ultimately, *that* is a sign of a "righteous nation"—that its laws may change in time because they become unnecessary due to a massive change in hearts.

PROPHETS GIVE AN ALTERNATIVE NARRATIVE

You absolutely *do* need lobbyists in the political arena who speak a plumbline of righteousness, but you must also steward the responsibility of teaching the church how Christianity (the Kingdom of God) actually works—which means not just influencing, but also building an alternative narrative to the one we have right now.

Case Study:
TEEN PREGNANCY IN HAWAII
I once heard Landa Cope, the brilliant YWAM scholar and teacher, recounting a story from Hawaii that illustrates the inherent complexities of relying on the law to institute moral change at

a societal level, and the need for us to be more holistic and less single-issue focused as a church.

At one time Hawaii had one of the highest teen pregnancy rates in the United State—hundreds and hundreds of teen pregnancies. A concerted campaign managed to significantly address this issue and the teenage pregnancy rate began to drop. Incredibly, teen pregnancy was reduced by nearly 80 percent between 1991 and 2020 and the number of abortions in Hawaii were halved. However, the community was shocked to discover that the rates for child abuse went up by 300 percent in the following years. Cope remarked that, "the issue is not just saving the baby—the baby may be dead from child abuse if you don't somehow change the culture, the culture of violence, of incest (which is rampant), absent husbands, powerless women…"

Don't misunderstand the point that Landa Cope is making. Reducing teen pregnancies and abortion statistics is of course encouraging, but we may be sweeping a whole lot of other problems under the rug if we don't also model a different culture and think about cultural change, more than simply political change. To change the culture of violence, of absent fathers, of disem-powered mothers, is the role of a church who understands heart transformation.

By all means, it *is* a positive thing to have a flag that you're carrying, waving, and working on—in other words, to have an issue that drives and motivates you—but understand it in the context of Scripture. For example, if you do manage to repeal the abortion laws, you have not made your nation more righteous or more acceptable to God, because *you didn't change a single heart in the process.* In fact, the reality may well actually turn out to be that you, by using law to enforce one issue, you have merely shifted a set of horrendous issues to somewhere else—and in doing so have angered and shut down the love of Jesus Christ to the very sector of society you were hoping to win.

Perhaps we are happy to be militant, polit-ical lobbyists because we are enamored with heavy-handed domination (which panders to our empire, territorial ego) and, on some days, to our love of justice and righteousness. Has angry pro-test at a distance become easier than the effort of vulnerability required in the conversations that

> **Are we enraging people by only being known for what we are against, rather than winning them with the limitless possibilities of transformation that are available in the Kingdom of God?**

move people to choose Christ? If our love of righteousness and justice is outworked in a brutal way toward our fellow citizens, do we really know what righteousness and justice are? Are we enraging people by only being known for what we are *against*, rather than winning them with the limitless possibilities of transformation that are available in the Kingdom of God?

I strongly suggest that if the unborn baby really means something to you, then law change will be quite far down your personal list of priorities to action. Don't tell me that the unborn baby means anything to you if your only activity on it has been your vote.

10

HOW GOD DISCIPLINES NATIONS

Politics is always downstream of culture.

—Andrew Breitbart,
American Conservative Journalist

OUR CULTURE DICTATES OUR POLITICS

The church is a signpost toward Jesus and His Kingdom. It models family and the success of family as a cultural model and impactor. It shows what transformation is possible from the inside out and, by demonstration, from the nature of how we do communities. Our approach should be utterly compelling and winsome—it is revolutionary rather than contemporary.

Culture always comes first. Culture dictates what politics does. Politics *never* dictates culture!

If we assume that nations change because of politics, then we open the door to a dangerous version of prophecy that is motivated by politicization rather than the Kingdom of God.

Politicians win votes because people like that they reflect the cultural values that they already inhabit. Politics is a game played mostly by individuals who want to become elected by speaking the rhetoric of the populace back to them, thus securing votes. In other words, nations get the leaders they deserve. No politician would have changed the gender laws had that culture not already been there, developing among the people.

We are foolish to think that our voting and the laws our politicians make is how righteousness comes to a nation. Once we have partnered with the misguided assumption that nations change because their politics are brilliant, then we open the door to a dangerous version of prophecy that is motivated by politicization rather than the Kingdom of God. The Kingdom of God is more revolutionary than the Western nations like to acknowledge!

A radical church with revolution in its bones will impact one life at a time, the "righteousness level" of a nation. It is *never* that strong politics equal a strong nation, nor that strong politics equals a righteous nation.

HOW DOES GOD DISCIPLINE NATIONS?

There are times when God is in "course-correction mode" with a nation. For instance, He may be dealing with their pride or letting them walk out the consequences of their sin so that they may call out for Him afresh. As prophetic people, what should we be on the lookout for?

- God allows oppressive rulers to become agents of His righteous anger.
- In the Bible, regimes like Rome, Babylon, and Persia are all brought into power, and He trains the righteous remnant amid threat, oppression, and exile.
- Scripturally, the training of a righteous remnant rarely happens in times of blessing!

And this is also, consistently, the case in our *own* lives. We learn more in our failure than in our success. We learn more in the pressing than in the blessing.

The training of a righteous remnant rarely happens in times of blessing!

All the way through the Old Testament, as nations invade and punish Israel, God's anger can be measured by what sort of government He allows to be in positions of authority. This is always to birth a better church.

God has, and does, allow corrupt rulers to accomplish His purposes. It does not mean that He endorses them. It does mean that He is the King of kings and will use what is necessary to train His people.

As the story of the Hebrew Bible progresses, Babylon invades and takes Jerusalem, Persia invades and takes Babylon, Greece invades and takes Persia, and then the Greeks are overwhelmed in the book of Daniel. This is not a comment on who is a better people group, this is just how God chooses to outwork correction and the relentless pursuit in His heart to get His people back into dependence on Him.

Whenever a nation "deifies" itself, speaks of its own greatness—or even calls itself great—whenever it elevates itself or abuses its power, God will allow unsavory leaders in, to teach it a lesson (or He will relocate the dominant international power away from that nation, or weaken its currency) and to stir up His bride in that nation to become ready. Therefore, it is very important to note that you often get the leaders who are right for what God is doing in your nation, rather than who and what you think you would prefer.

Prophets, who we get as our leaders is really, really *not* about meeting our own personal comforts! God is not, first and foremost, interested in the cost of our fuel, our taxes, or whatever else is the political or economic issue of the day! Therefore, we do not rage against governments as our first response to them. Rather, we should ask questions including:

- How now do we radically extend the Kingdom of God when we are not comforted and backed by those in power?
- How do we grow into Christian biblical maturity because our leaders have produced an oppressive atmosphere?
- How do we best grow under persecution?
- Have we lost the ability to take correction and seek maturity as a church community?

> **You often get the leaders who are right for what God is doing in your nation, rather than who you would prefer.**

- Have we favored a spirit of criticism rather than cultivating an attitude of learning, and so our oppression worsens?

God has a history of worsening situations until He gets the results He wants—think back to Egypt's plagues. God allows situations to frustrate us so that we may be forced to produce something He cannot currently find in us and stretch us until we become the Kingdom of God.

Jesus Christ is predominantly interested in the condition of His bride. A healthy bride will mean a healthy nation. If there is a political leader I hate, perhaps he or she is the very leader who will make the church in my land waken up to build the Kingdom of God! God is coming for a spotless bride, not a spotless nation.

King Jesus marries His bride then destroys and rebuilds the earth. The end of the story is a clear Psalm 2 smashing of the nations to pieces. This should make it very clear to us, if it isn't already, that our nations are not the Kingdom of God! The Kingdom of God finds its full expression, its full out-working through the *ecclesia*. The Kingdom of God

God is coming for a spotless bride, not a spotless nation.

does not find its full expression in the political process.

> **We do not put our hope in politics and politicians.**

THE FUTILITY OF POLITICS

God's Kingdom can never be fully implemented at the political level because the political system is part of the world's systems, which ultimately will be destroyed. For sure, politics, government, and civil justice can—and most certainly should—be used for good, but politics does not usher in the return of Jesus Christ, nor does it ever replace the church's responsibility to build the Kingdom of God. Therefore, we do not put our hope in politics and politicians.

We are guilty of seeking the government or the politics that we expect will build the Kingdom of God for us. Then when elections shock us and don't go our way, and when we feel robbed by a result, we rage constantly for years because our flawed measurement tells us that we are in a worse place. We say, "Poor church!"

Rather, the response should always be, "Your Kingdom come!" For surely light shines brightest in a dark place. Instead, the correct response is,

"Thank You, Jesus, that You don't make mistakes and that You have given back to *us*, Your people, the responsibility that we had delegated away to politics."

When things are hostile and even seem to go horrifically against the people of God, we raise a prayer of strength for one another, protection over each other's lives, and gratitude that Jesus is forcing the church back into accountability—because we should appreciate that it is nobody else's job to lead people to Jesus but ours.

Prayer

Write on my heart anew, Father God. Help me understand what You want for Your church. Keep me from assumptions and lead me into fresh wisdom and revelation. I cry out for the mind of Christ, that I might think His thoughts, and know His ways. In Jesus's name, amen.

PROPHESYING TO NATIONS

Here are some "top tip" questions to ask yourself prior to prophesying about your nation. Ask God where your nation is in terms of:

> **God, is my nation in about to go into exile, is it in the middle of exile, or are we coming out of exile?**

- Is it a day of justice and judgment, or a day of blessing and liberty?
- Are you in exile, being stripped and shaken?
- Are you in a season of punishment?
- Where is God's mercy and compassion to be found?
- What are the conditions God puts on your actions to see His presence?
- Are you in wild blessing and increase, stepping into promised land?
- Jesus, what is the key lesson that You want my nation to be made aware of?

Scripture defines peoples as being either in *pre-exilic*, *during-exile*, and *post-exilic* eras. Therefore, we should be asking these sorts of questions about our nation. A prophet should always know how God is preparing the bride in that nation and what He requires from her in terms of action.

11

CULTURAL PERSPECTIVES

If you have not chosen the Kingdom
of God first, it will in the end make no
difference what you have chosen instead.

—William Law

OUR BACKYARD PERSPECTIVES

How we navigate the world around us and how
we view the world is massively influenced by our
culture.

The way we see things depends on our life
experience, geography, nation, and where we
stand in society. As I described in the Introduction,
the hostile political environment of my childhood
gave me a totally skewed vision of Catholicism.
The Protestant community truly believed that a
Roman Catholic could never be a Christian. "Come
out from among them and be separate," was the

biblical phrase given by the Protestant community to ensure we never associated with Catholics.

Likewise, your upbringing will be responsible for your cultural and political indoctrination. You must know that this exists. Without a shadow of a doubt, your political opinion will have been influenced by your upbringing.

We see through a "backyard perspective." We are shaped by our culture, that of our own backyard, before we even think to question it. You will not have escaped this. Yes, even you! It is why we need people from other cultures and nations to come and chat through how they see our cultural norms and ideologies with their outside eyes. Jesus will "make wrongs right" in a way that I don't understand because I'm biased and partial. I believe that we are in danger of missing Jesus's actions in our midst because of our personal prejudice.

The great danger of this is that we see God as *we* are. God is viewed through our non-objectivity.

The Bible expresses that we see dimly:

> *When I was a child, I used to speak like a child, think like a child, reason like a child; when I became a man, I did away with childish things. For now we*

see in a mirror dimly, but then face to face; now I know in part, but then I will know fully just as I also have been fully known (1 Corinthians 13:11-12 NASB).

We have to be honest and accept that something is clouded in us, and we are prone to fanciful nonsense— which is, in essence, idolatry. The need to repetitively examine our own hearts and use the sword of the Lord to divide

Your political opinion is influenced by your upbringing.

between biblical reality and cultural idolatry will need to grow into a lifestyle for us. Jesus is not us on our best day. He is not us dressed up!

Those of us who are prophets and leaders must especially, and rigorously, require ourselves to lay hands on our own eyes and ask for skewed vision to be burnt away. Even walking out a prophetic act of taking off cultural lenses, as part of prayerful repentance is a good spiritual discipline. Why don't you do that right now?

Prayer

[Put your hands on your eyes] *Father God, You are holy. You are high above all things, and I exalt You. Have mercy on me, for Your thoughts have not been my thoughts, and neither have Your ways been my ways. Forgive me of my ideologies that are not of You. I repent of my cultural opinions, where they have blinded, skewed, dimly reflected, or shadowed what You were trying to say to me, or do through my life. I take off my cultural lenses again, so that I might see more clearly. I unblock my ears of my own politics, biases, opinions, and dogmas. May I be a purified vessel and hear You better, for the sake of those You have called me to. Holy Spirit, help me to be more like Jesus Christ. Speak Lord, I'm listening. Amen.*

OUR CULTURAL VALUES

THE IDOLS OF "ISMS"

Ideologies are everywhere in the culture around us and you and I hold dearly to at least one—but probably many—whether we are aware of them or not. They're the ideas, beliefs, or philosophies that we (and the people who matter to us) hold dearly. An ideology is sometimes easy to spot because it will (usually) end with "-ism." For example, in the world of politics and economics you might have heard of ideologies such as capitalism, socialism, conservatism, libertarianism, individualism, collectivism, nationalism, and globalism. Though many of these ideas compete with each other, they sometimes overlap and you're likely to know people who hold on to at least one of these ideals from among your wider circle of friendship. Of course, in our history there have been even more extreme political ideologies that are now rare (in the West at least): communism, fascism, Nazism.

But ideologies are not only political. They can be moral too: racism, moral liberalism, progressivism, fundamentalism, feminism, and environmentalism are some other examples found in society. And even our religious life has a subset of ideologies within it; for example, Protestantism, Roman Catholicism, Pentecostalism, Presbyterianism, Complementarianism, Egalitarianism, and Pre-Millennialism—to name but a few!

All ideologies have their own *sotierology* (salvation story) and *eschatology* (end goal). In other words, we believe our particular ideology has a way to save us all, and a final vision of how it will look for the world. Adherents to one ideology or another become possessed by the pursuit of a utopian end goal, and so "the end justifies the means." As a result, the world has witnessed some horrendous consequences as peoples and powers have relentlessly pursued their favored ideology. One political philosopher summed up the danger of this as, *"The relevant question thus becomes, not whether the state is acting justly, but whether it is acting so as eventually to achieve justice. Under the latter approach, justice becomes an ideal located somewhere in the future, and whatever one does in the here and now is permissible if it serves the attainment of this goal."*

> Any ideology that is not in submission ultimately to the good news of the Kingdom of Jesus Christ, is a false hope, and can very quickly become an idol to us. We should be very careful whenever we become passionate about one particular "ism" over another! All ideologies fall short of the full glory of God.

Values differ widely around the globe. For example, the West is obsessed with its individual empowerments and rights, but the global South and Asia tend to have a communitarian approach, rather than a libertarian approach. Some nations and cultures value honor and respect more than others. Our politics reflect these cultural norms.

We are all in some form of indoctrination, therefore reading Scripture cover-to-cover and in huge chunks will inform and reform the priorities of the Kingdom in us. After all, if we had been more biblically inquisitive and open to challenge, we would not have been so shocked by our God and some of what He has allowed to happen in our lives and nation. God is incredibly okay with our deep uncomfortableness—because His value system is not ours.

If we had been more biblically open to challenge, we would not have been so shocked by some of what God has allowed to happen.

We tend to come to Scripture by pulling apart verses out of context. You can almost make Scripture say anything if you do not pursue its full story arc, in context.

But the need to think as God thinks and feel as God feels is imperative. Becoming more aligned to God than to our political opinion is the necessary journey of today. We are predominantly and primarily citizens of the Kingdom of God before we are Canadian, or British, or American.

But you are a chosen people, a royal priesthood, a holy nation, God's special possession, that you may declare the praises of him who called you out of darkness into his wonderful light (1 Peter 2:9 NIV).

You are in the nation of God before you are anything else. You don't just follow the Savior, you follow the King! You are now part of a civilization headed up and led by Almighty God Himself.

Therefore, you have more in common with a Christian living in Asia, than you do with a non-believer living in the house next to you. We as followers of Christ are the family of God together, the Kingdom of God working to change lives.

This really pushes at our racist tendencies, for we all have nations that we prefer over other nations. Yet the nation you like the least *will* have Christian family members in it who should be more aligned to you than your non-Christian work colleagues, for they will share values and a culture far superior to any the world offers! We dare not slander them, for we are all in communion together with God.

THE GOSPEL OF THE KINGDOM

Our recent decades have slid us into the limited "gospel of salvation" rather than the full "gospel of the Kingdom," which has resulted in a challenging journey for us to be submitted to anything we do not like.

The nation you like the least will have family members in it who are more aligned to you than your non-Christian work colleagues.

The gospel of salvation is a well-intended but misplaced half-story. It means that you came to Jesus for the purpose of Heaven (getting into Heaven when you die), rather than the purpose of the Kingdom. The gospel of the Kingdom of God is scandalous! We need a reconstructing of our understanding about the difference between the "gospel of salvation," where we make Jesus our personal Savior—and the gospel of the Kingdom of God, where we submit to Him as the Ruler of all.

> **Pledging allegiance, or having strong, earthly, nationalistic tendencies is a place of dangerous unseating of the premier place that the Kingdom of God should have in your heart.**

Yes, of course, Jesus is absolutely our Savior, but He is also Lord, and He is King of kings. Consequently, the gospel of the Kingdom is not about making Jesus the Lord of your life. He is already the crowned ruler of heaven and earth. So, the issue is not one of making Jesus Lord—He already is Lord!

Therefore, the issue of our salvation is about you and me submitting to His already-established Lordship. At salvation, it should never be only an individualistically minded, "Jesus, I allow you into my heart to look after me, and then, bit-by-bit, you can have the throne of my life." Rather, it is, "Jesus, I completely surrender to your universal rulership!" He does, of course, individually save us and becomes one with us in spirit (1 Corinthians 6:17) when we repent, believe, and acknowledge Him as Lord... but it is so much more than a salvation transaction!

At this moment, you did not just receive a personal Savior; you chose to follow a King—a King with a holy nation and a government (ecclesia) that you became part of and subject to before anything else. Therefore, pledging allegiance to a country or anything else, or having strong, earthly, nationalistic tendencies is a place of dangerous unseating of the premier place that the Kingdom of God should have in your heart.

When you are absolutely certain that your heart has understood this—then, and only then, do I think that you have permission to prophesy into politics, and not before.

12

WHOSE SIDE IS GOD ON?

"Sir, my concern is not whether God is on our side; my greatest concern is to be on God's side, for God is always right."

—Abraham Lincoln,
U.S. President

Completely shockingly, the Bible does not endorse any particular form of organized government. It does not say monarchy is best, nor dictatorship, nor a republic. Although we have personal preferences, the fact is that multiple types of human government can facilitate God's purpose to the earth. Remember, God is a specialist at bringing order out of chaos. We will be glad that some nation's realities are not our realities.

God is not even necessarily pro-democracy. God can even get His candidate in on the back of corruption and fraudulence!

MAN'S RULING SYSTEMS

Human forms of rulership are easily spotted by the ending "-*archy*" or "-*cracy*." For example, monarchy (rule of a monarch, a single person), aristocracy (rule of the higher class), democracy (rule of the people), oligarchy (rule of the few), or theocracy (rule of religious leaders).

Some governmental regimes are strongly authoritarian (such as the People's Republic of China—a state ruled by a single party) and when the government extends their rule into people's daily tasks and rules, this is known as totalitarian government (e.g., North Korea). The Islamic Republic of Iran is a theocracy (ruled by religious leaders).

It can be easy for those of us in so-called democracies like the United Kingdom (Parliamentary Democracy) or the USA (Republic) to assume that our models are truly representative and therefore somehow "perfect." But this is naïve; consider, for example, the millions of pounds or dollars spent on political campaigns lobbying. To say that our political system is free from corruption is delusional!

In any case, the places where the Kingdom of God seems to be expanding most rapidly and dramatically are those nations where persecution and economic crisis abounds; there is no correlation between democracy and salvation!

Romans 13 is such an important scripture that it is worth quoting a large portion of the chapter:

> Let everyone be subject to the governing authorities, for there is no authority except that which God has established. The authorities that exist have been established by God. Consequently, whoever rebels against the authority is rebelling against what God has instituted, and those who do so will bring judgment on themselves. For rulers hold no terror for those who do right, but for those who do wrong. Do you want to be free from fear of the one in authority? Then do what is right and you will be commended. For the one in authority is God's servant for your good. But if you do wrong, be

afraid, for rulers do not bear the sword for no reason. They are God's servants, agents of wrath to bring punishment on the wrongdoer. Therefore, it is necessary to submit to the authorities, not only because of possible punishment but also as a matter of conscience. This is also why you pay taxes, for the authorities are God's servants, who give their full time to governing. Give to everyone what you owe them: if you owe taxes, pay taxes; if revenue, then revenue; if respect, then respect; if honor, then honor **(Romans 13:1-7 NIV).**

Paul makes it very clear that we must honor the structure of government and the leadership wherever we find ourselves. By all means, if you can leverage the political system, do so, but retain the characteristics of the Kingdom of God.

WHOSE SIDE? NEITHER!

Joshua 5 describes a marvelous encounter between Joshua and a man with a drawn sword:

...Joshua went up to him and asked, "Are you for us or for our enemies?" "Neither," he replied, "but as commander of the army of the Lord I have now come." Then Joshua fell face down to the ground in reverence, and asked him, "What message does my Lord have for his servant?" (Joshua 5:13-14 NIV).

When Joshua met the Angel of the Lord his first question is, "Whose side are you on?" The answer is, "No one!" God is only on God's side. We biblically fail when we assign God to a side or to a political party, because that means that we are assigning righteousness to a political party. Political parties are not the *ecclesia*, they are part of the world system and are most certainly *not* the righteousness of God.

We're not supposed to be defiantly left wing, or right wing. We are not supposed to be libertarian versus communitarian. We are supposed to be representatives of the government of God. God is

We biblically fail when we assign God to a side, or to a political party, because that means that we are assigning righteousness to a political party.

happy with your preferences, but He will not entertain your prejudices.

God is happy with your preferences, but He will not entertain your prejudices.

PROPHETS AND POLITICAL ALLEGIANCES

My personal desire would be that all senior prophetic leaders would have no party-political allegiance or affiliation, and to be muted in any display of their preference so that God can have spokesmen and spokeswomen who only ever align with what He says and how He wants His will communicated. As prophets, we do not lead people into what *we* want, we lead people into what God wants. Shepherds speak on behalf of the people, but prophets speak on behalf of God.

God can, and will, alarm us on occasions by asking us to prepare a people for an outcome that they will not like. I have watched this be an almost impossible task to do if you are consistently reinforcing your own preferences and how you think God *ought* to act in your nation. You are not even to be neutral—you are to be forcefully on the side of the King, whatever that looks like in an era!

Shepherds speak on behalf of the people, but prophets speak on behalf of God.

If your call is into the political arena then let that be celebrated and supported: gather the intercessors around you while you hold plumblines of truth, but do not prophesy out of your allegiance to a party. Do not turn your commentating, punditry, and intercession into a prophetic word that does irreparable damage to the people and to the reputation of the voice of God.

THE IMPACT OF CULTURAL AND POLITICAL BIAS

The impact of our cultural and political bias has been nothing short of the politicization of our faith and the stunting of the forward movement of the church. In the nations where we have a state church, the church has bowed the knee to the headship of death and to the headship of the systems of this world. State churches are in partnership agreements with the kingdoms of this world and ultimately these churches are diminishing, all while they increasingly become conduits for the death of truth. A dually aligned house cannot stand.

Many find these days challenging because of their underwhelm in church. We have been massively guilty of pausing reformation, and yet we should be in *constant* reformation as the people of God. But when you cannot see beyond your own man-made bias, all godly courage is lost, and with it the ability for transformation. We are in a reduced place, trapped in the boundaries of the world because we agreed to the success measurements of the world, over the Kingdom's measures of success. We are set up for worldly success, not Kingdom success and the possibilities of the limitless Kingdom of God are absent from us!

Reductionism—which is reducing our beliefs into small, defendable ideals, sound bites that don't encompass the fullness of truth, and the part-quoting of biblical verses to back ourselves—is not the model. Ultimately, political bias destroys relationships, as it requires us to defend a small version of unresolved truth. It makes us defensive. Defensive people make enemies. Defensive *nations* make enemies!

And so, people of the Kingdom, we must hold loosely our cultural and political bias, and our inherited orthodoxy, and

Do not turn your commentating, punditry, and intercession into a prophetic word.

not get stuck in certain decades, weaponizing our nostalgia about the past or particular "half-truths." Even in eternity we will always keep learning about God! But right now we are arrogant enough to believe that we have understood truth, which is like saying, "I fully grasp God." A comprehended or understood God is no God at all.

HAVE CONVERSATIONS

A rich part of the Hebraic tradition is the idea that one, seemingly inconsequential, human being may be trusted by God to have key, fresh, insight into how Scripture should be interpreted and applied. Therefore, Jewish people have always highly prioritized conversations about truth. We have lost this art in the church and have preferred our argumentative defensiveness. We have cast away the concept of being sharpened—across political parties, across denominational boundaries, and certainly across international boundaries. But defensive people cannot easily steward revelation, as revelation is largely about change and transformation. True revelation rarely seeks to tell you, "You have no need to change!"

Prophets, when you lose the ability to be sharpened, you are in a very dangerous place. When you only want or give diluted, over-edited, revelation, you rip from the body of Christ the ability to keep in time with what God is doing. You prevent them from getting to know and understand the Father heart of God, who is always working things for the good of those who love Him—even if that is difficult in a given moment.

We must hold loosely our cultural and political bias, and our inherited orthodoxy, and not get stuck in certain decades, weaponizing our nostalgia about the past or particular "half-truths."

13

HOW DO WE ACT NOW?

The future doesn't just happen. We are
building it, and we are building it all the time.

—Hannah Fry

I believe in the balance between
dreaming and building.

—Neri Oxman

The Bible richly encourages us to either build the Kingdom of God or to influence the kingdoms of this world. Although they directly relate to one another they have different emphases. Are you a builder of the Kingdom, or are you an influencer of the world systems?

HOW MUCH INFLUENCE CAN I HAVE?

The Old Testament model of transformation is based around the question, "How much influence can I have?" The leading lights of this are Esther, Daniel, and Joseph. The general direction of travel for these transformers is to get as high as you can in order to shape and influence culture.

As the people of God, this seems to be nearly the only thought that we have about how society changes, and it is *so* limited! We have become absolutely driven by rising high and getting close to power—and most certainly this concept of being an influencer is massively shaping our youth.

> **We have become absolutely driven by rising high and getting close to power.**

This is very much the thought behind the influencing of the different defined sections of society. It looks at high-functioning experts going into Hollywood, the same into business, and to education, and so—until every facet of national life has a believer in it, at or near the top, bringing truth. It is valid, but it is only one part of the biblical picture.

WHAT CAN I BUILD?

The New Testament model is very significantly different and is based around the question, "What can I build?" First, it is about building transformation into the individual life—for the Kingdom of God is built in people.

Jesus said, *"The coming of the kingdom of God is not something that can be observed, nor will people say, 'Here it is,' or 'There it is,' because the kingdom of God is in your midst"* (Luke 17:20-21 NIV). *"In your midst"* implies that the Kingdom of Heaven is in the middle of you, and it will flow out of you if you are led by the Holy Spirit.

The Kingdom flows from you as you connect with the King—His Spirit, His realm, His dimension, His values, and His priorities. The Kingdom of God is a realm, a spiritual domain, it is *not* a place, or a geography, or a nation. And so, a Kingdom Builder is not seeking the domination or control of another empire. A Kingdom Builder is deeply connected to the understanding of spiritual realms, and to the King who is individually received, and yet His values are shared by all of us who believe.

The New Testament progresses the concepts of a world system that will be judged, repeating over and over the prophecy of the fall of Babylon as a metaphor for the kingdoms of this world. The world system is not sustainable; and, in time, the kingdoms of this world will be replaced. Education, politics, business, entertainment, and so on, are part of the kingdoms of the world. The New Testament urges building the Kingdom of God (it is the very core of the Lord's prayer—*your* Kingdom come is not only about the future date of the return of Jesus, it is a prayer for the here and now) and creating systems that people can migrate to that infect and interface with the world.

You are supposed to build something that evacuates the world system—we are building the Kingdom of God outside of the world system.

You are supposed to build something that evacuates the world system—yes, you leave some to keep influencing in the world, but on the whole, we are building the Kingdom of God outside of the world system. This is why the Kingdom of God sounds treasonous to world leaders and is dangerous to all other powers.

"I will build my church," the great statement of Jesus in Matthew 16, sets a new tone. Paul gets

this, and in 1 Corinthians chapter 3, he calls himself the master builder:

> According to the grace of God which was given to me, like a wise master builder I laid a foundation, and another is building on it. ...If any man's work which he has built on it remains, he will receive a reward (1 Corinthians 3:10,14 NASB).

For example, we build an education system, not for the exclusive use of the people of God, but rather as a standard of the best education, with a wide-open door to everyone. In Britain we started this and then we gave schools back to the government to run—we foolishly handed education back to a demonically rooted system. But we still think it should listen to us and be run by our biblical moral code, with Bible reading in the classroom, and are surprised when we are rejected!

We are supposed to own and build television studios that tell wholesome, moral stories. We are to build the new banking systems to depopulate the world banking's system. We use our energy to build first—predominantly—*hearts*, and then structures.

SOME ARE CALLED TO INFLUENCE

Some *are* called to influence—which is predominantly a dismantling mandate—to tear down, by proximity, the world systems. This does require faithful presence, because if you move out from being salt and light in the world system it will very quickly revert back to its demonic roots. After all, it has been built on a foundation to honor satan (that's why satan could offer it to Jesus at His temptation).

There is an inherent danger in becoming too focused on influence, and we saw this play out in the politics of recent years. Because we, the church, were more wired for influence than for building, we became unable to cope with the notion that a non-Christian government could be in a position of authority and that could somehow still be okay. We panicked and partnered with fear and distrust.

Likewise, we prophets had become so wired for influence in government ("top-down influence is the only way a nation is changed") that we could not conceive of prophesying according to God. Therefore, we felt we had no choice but to prophesy (wrongly) that the Christians would—*must*—get the senior political jobs in the nation!

We had become so wired for influence in government that we felt we had no choice but to prophesy (wrongly) that the Christians would get the senior political jobs in the nation.

One day the world's systems—Babylon—are going to end. They will be destroyed at the hand of Jesus Christ, and His unshakable Kingdom will completely replace them. God hates the world's systems with a passion because they keep people away from His Son.

TRUE KINGDOM BUILDING

I invite you to find out and know whether you are predominantly a builder, or an influencer. There is a grace on building that I don't think we have fully tapped into. In the church we have used any building grace that we did have to build either empire or mega churches. In doing so, we have become more interested in influence, losing a biblical thrust to create Kingdom of God structures. Within politics and governments, we surrendered a building mantle for a vote, and believed that one vote on one day would be blessed as if we were actually taking responsibility for our nation.

PRAYER

Lord Jesus, You are my King. May we love Your Kingdom, how You govern, and how You work, more than anything else in the systems of the world.

14

HOW DO YOU VOTE?

The only freedom which deserves
the name, is that of pursuing our
own good in our own way.

—John Stuart Mill,
1806-73, English Philosopher and Economist

For none of us lives to himself, and
no one dies to himself. For if we live,
we live to the Lord; and if we die, we
die to the Lord. Therefore, whether
we live or die, we are the Lord's.

—Paul,
Letter to the Romans 14:7-8 NKJV

LISTEN TO THE HOLY SPIRIT

When we go to the ballot box, visiting the polling station in our local or national elections, we should resist the temptation to be driven by our preconceived ideas and our assumptions. Instead, talk to God about your preferences and ask Him what candidate *He* wants you to back. And be open to not liking the answer! You may not understand what God is doing, but as a subject

The Kingdom of God grows amongst any political system.

of the King, this is the training ground where you will discover if you really have the capacity to, "love not your own life."

> *And they overcame* [the accuser] *because of the blood of the Lamb and because of the word of their testimony, and they did not love their life even when faced with death* (Revelation 12:11 NASB).

Remember too, that God operates in an arc of multigenerational timings, way beyond our four- or five-year political cycles. Overall, the church is not asked by God (or even required by God) to vote one way or another, nor to back a specific system of government. The Kingdom of God does not require your preferred political system in order to grow—it grows amongst *any* system.

THE "GOD" OF LIBERTY

Ultimately, our Western ideology loves the driving master of "liberty." Liberty is undeniably a god for almost every inhabitant of the world. However, in complete liberty, as defined by the kingdoms of this world, you have absolute freedom—without moral boundary or constraint—to be who you want to be. Once you can be whoever or whatever you want to be, there is no requirement for a Savior, nor God, because none of your sense of self is perceived as being in error. You see yourself as sinless and without need of salvation.

Therefore, absolute freedom is moral anarchy! Any people who enshrine liberty, but without the biblical definition that *it is the freedom to be like Christ*, will have lost biblical morality. A promiscuous society will have liberty-outside-of-Christ as its driving motivation—where each of its citizens become gods. Liberty-outside-of-Christ is the mascot, slogan, constitution, motivation, and lifestyle aim of a society given over to self-worship. Congratulations, you have made yourself god!

It is hard to know at what point a people fall into the horror of Romans 1, where God "gives them over" to their sin:

Therefore God gave them over in the sinful desires of their hearts to sexual impurity for the degrading of their bodies with one another. They exchanged the truth about God for a lie, and worshiped and served created things rather than the Creator—who is forever praised. Amen (Romans 1:24-25 NIV).

A promiscuous society will have liberty-outside-of-Christ as its driving motivation—where each of its citizens become gods.

Here in Romans 1, God chooses a moment to abandon people to their passions, where their perceived liberty becomes enslavement, and they become their own emperors—losing all sense of the need for King Jesus. We would call this a "pre-Christian," entirely secular, society. Therefore, expect God be extreme in how He deals with these people. Be prepared for it not to be comfortable—and for your choice at the ballot box to be, on occasions, a small part of a much bigger picture of what your nation requires.

In other words, God's plan to deal with your nation might involve your nation being governed

Expect God be extreme in how He deals with people who are given over to their sin. Be prepared for it not to be comfortable.

by tyrants who you don't much like, to bring the people to repentance and the acknowledgment of their need of the Savior. (Of course, that doesn't mean that you need to endorse tyrants and back tyranny—the first-century church never endorsed Nero or his mark!)

We can have all the improvements of science, modernity, entertainment, and wealth, but when the holiness of God is disregarded, He steps in and obstructs a nation's haughty ambitions, in foundational ways. The Western liberty-oriented nations are perhaps in the greatest slavery that the world has ever known. They have committed crimes against their own welfare by the love of self-liberation, their dislike of anybody's will apart from their own—and especially their dislike of the will of God. *"This is the verdict: Light has come into the world, but people loved darkness instead of light because their deeds were evil"* (John 3:19 NIV).

Watch the wrath of God come to the dictatorial tyrants who enslave, but also to the foolishness of us in the West, for we have enslaved ourselves. In light of this, you must see that your vote is playing a game in the kingdom of this world when all the while the Kingdom of God is working to a much, much bigger agenda. Know and understand that discomfort, persecution, and wars, though not easy for us to embrace (nor something to be rashly sought out), may now come to sharpen us and our fellow men and women, as God's way to win us back.

WHAT IF YOU *ARE* CALLED TO SERVE IN POLITICS?

Much of this book has been written to prophets and prophetic people, those who are called to reveal the voice of God to their communities, cities, and nations (that's probably you!).

However, you may be specifically called to serve in politics and civil government. If you are, be blessed! Serve to the best of your ability and be a light in the darkness. The following are some top tips to bear in mind if this is your call:

> **The Kingdom of God is working to a much, much bigger agenda.**

- Always heed Jesus's words to beware the leaven of Herod and the Pharisees.

In other words, beware of political and religious spirits and how they seek to pollute everything, often working together to an end that is counter to the Kingdom of God.

- Don't be seduced into believing that politics, politicians, and political power have all the answers!

- Ask yourself, "Am I being a light in a dark place by my thoughts, deeds and actions, or am I trying to leverage the political process to enact laws that I mistakenly think will usher in the Kingdom of God?"

- Remember that you are serving in Babylon. We are not the Israelites in the Promised Land; we are citizens of the Kingdom of God, sojourning in Babylon. Our goal is therefore not to perfect our nation or the world but to offer God's perspective, a better way, and allow society a choice simply, humbly, and excellently.

- We can't beat or force the lost into understanding God's values of morality and political justice.

- Jesus's followers were surprised that their Messiah came like a servant more than a political or military ruler. Are you trying to style Jesus in the image of the former, or the latter?

- We can't impose Kingdom ethics on the world, but we can call people into the Kingdom. Nevertheless, we can have great influence as we are salt and light, offering alternatives to the lies of satan, who is lawless.

- Don't ever be lured into thinking, "God is with us, but not with them" when it comes to your political affiliations. Remember, God is on no side but His own.

- You probably have more in common than you realize with a believer who is on the opposite side of the political spectrum to you because of your shared Christ-centered, Kingdom ideology and values. In fact, you probably have more in common with your fellow Kingdom citizen than you do with someone in your own political party who is not a believer!

- Therefore, seek to work on cross-party, bipartisan projects wherever possible. Beware of partisanship and tribalism and instead look for joint solutions to civil justice issues.

- Examine your motivations with the Holy Spirit. Ask questions such as:

  ◆ "Am I seeing the world through a lens of fear?"

  ◆ "Am I regarding this person or that person as a threat to be eliminated, rather than as a fellow image-bearer of God who can be engaged with?"

  ◆ And "Is my belief that I am fighting for truth so consuming me that I am justifying hatred or a lack of compassion and love?"

As believers in the Kingdom of God, as followers of Jesus Christ, we absolutely should be prepared to speak truth to power and to call for higher standards of justice, righteousness, and goodness. We who study Scripture by the lens of the Holy Spirit have a great deal to contribute to the political discourse. It is simply not right to say, "We don't do God," as the spokesman for former Prime Minister Tony Blair once did, referring to the party's fear that speaking about faith might damage their electoral hopes.

We don't withdraw from society, as the Anabaptists did. Christians *can* be politically involved and be a force for good, as Christian leaders such as William Wilberforce and many others have demonstrated over the centuries. Believers *can* run for political office and serve in government.

However, remember that governments of all kinds tend to work best when they have the consent of the governed—the people who choose you to serve them. If you seek change that the people you serve don't want, you are going to have a tough time trying to impose your views, your faith, and your morality on them! We must always know that hearts are only truly, eternally changed by relationship with Jesus—by our prophecies, not by our political party, economic ideologies, or our own preferences.

Prophets, you must speak truth from a purified, untainted reading of Scripture, by the illumination of the Holy Spirit.

WHEN IT COMES TO VOTING, DON'T BE SELFISH

God doesn't need us to look the same or have identical opinions about everything. Even the twelve tribes of Israel had different characteristics but were still considered God's children; and as I once heard someone say, "It wasn't the fact that Cain was meat eating and Abel was an agrarian farmer that offended God." There may be more than one way to solve a political, economic, or social problem, and the fact that another might have a different viewpoint from you is not necessarily a sign of a deeper flaw in their moral character or in their capacity to see reality for what it is!

In God's eyes, my vote is not the most important vote. In fact, my vote is nearly always a selfish vote, motivated by my own personal desires, needs, and fears. But in a democracy where everyone is allowed to vote, it is good and responsible to cast a vote and be part of the process.

God will bless a nation that allows all its citizens a fair and just say in how they are governed. So have your say! But remember that, from God's perspective, He cares more that the marginalized and oppressed have a voice. Jesus is not a big fan of those who press home their advantages in order to protect their own interests. Perhaps "loving your neighbor as yourself" means you ensuring that your neighbor gets an opportunity to cast their vote and be represented by who they want to be represented by, ahead of your own chance to vote. So, if you know a community, an area, a people group, or a person who is not currently able, or is hindered from voting, for whatever reason, do what you can to help them cast their vote—even if it is opposite to how you will vote. I believe God will bless you for doing so!

Jesus is not a big fan of those who press home their advantages in order to protect their own interests.

HOW DO WE BEHAVE IN TIMES OF WAR?

Conflict is on the increase in these days. The fire of our political discourse has become so heated that even family members have turned on family members. Our social media echo chambers only serve to fan the flames of tribalism that lead to civil division and even war. Prophets should prepare and behave differently in times of war than in times of peace. We should never be fearfully reactive to the threat of war, whether it be civil war within our national borders or a greater geo-political conflict. Jesus instructed His followers to stand firm because:

> *You will hear of wars and rumors of wars, but see to it that you are not alarmed. Such things must happen,*

but the end is still to come. Nation will rise against nation, and kingdom against kingdom. There will be famines and earthquakes in various places. All these are the beginning of birth pains. Then you will be handed over to be persecuted and put to death, and you will be hated by all nations because of me. At that time many will turn away from the faith and will betray and hate each other, and many false prophets will appear and deceive many people. Because of the increase of wickedness, the love of most will grow cold, but the one who stands firm to the end will be saved (Matthew 24:6-13 NIV).

Nevertheless, it can become so tempting to pick up our sword and join the fight (even if our "sword" is a pen, keyboard, or our own voice). Even Jesus's own disciples, who had been with Him as He ministered with love and compassion, quickly defaulted back to violence and human weapons—James and John (the "Sons of Thunder"), who asked to call down fire, and Peter, who took his sword to the temple guard. But in the end, each of these disciples chose differently. Following the way of Christ, they died as martyrs.

> *And having disarmed the powers and authorities, he made a public specta-cle of them, triumphing over them by the cross* (**Colossians 2:15 NIV**).

Our way, in the midst of war, is humility, love, compassion, no fear, and the taking away of the power of the enemy by laying down, by the power and love of God, our lives. Prophets, we must resist every notion and temptation to pick up the carnal weapons of the world and to join the fray, fighting back.

We are to love our enemies and pray for those who persecute us. Follow the example of our brothers and sisters in places like China, where the members of the underground church there are laying down their lives for each other *and* their enemies—it's a martyrdom movement that is reaping a great and mighty harvest!

Prophets, we must resist every notion and temptation to join the fray, fighting back.

Let Matthew 5 be our man-ifesto, and may we join with Paul in saying, *"I have been* crucified with Christ and I no longer live, but Christ lives in me. The life I now live in the body, I live by faith in the Son of God, who loved me and gave himself for me" (Galatians 2:20 NIV).

PRAYER

Heavenly Father, may Your Kingdom come and Your will be done, here on earth as it is in Heaven. Spirit of the Living God, fill me and lead me so that I might be a spokesperson and a demonstrator of Your Kingdom. Would You give me the gift of discernment that I might see and understand what is the culture of Heaven and also what is satan's—Babylon.

Lord Jesus, empower us, by Your Spirit, that we might be a purified, prophetic, end-times church, like the witnesses of Revelation 11. May we be truly salt and light. Jesus, I choose to step into my forerunning call, to be a revolutionary who does not seek to defend myself, my reputation, my own opinions, nor my own prejudices. I choose to seek and discover what You think about things, so that I and my fellow prophetic warriors can better reflect You in compassion and through transformative, Spirit-filled power.

May we, Your ecclesia, no longer look to man-made structures to rescue us, fund us, defend us, or legislate for us. We reject empire and domination and choose to lead godly lives as "foreigners and exiles" in the midst of Babylon. May we be a healthy, glowing bride in the midst of our nation.

Jesus, please forgive me when I have made my nation, my party, or my political preferences into an idol. Help me rid myself of any ideologies that are not of You and Your Kingdom.

Lord, have Your way in us. Have Your way in the nations. Amen!

FINALLY

Prophet, remember that God is always working on a vast plan of redemption, and He will do whatever it takes to secure us with Him, forever.

Appendix

SHEEP AND GOAT NATIONS

GOD WILL SEPARATE THE PEOPLE

In Chapter 7, I explained that there is no concept in the Bible of "sheep nations" (good, godly states) and "goat nations" (rebellious, idolatrous countries). You may have heard contrary teaching to this. Perhaps you've prayed or declared that your nation might be a "sheep nation" and not a "goat nation." The misconception that salvation might come through national identity or birthright is based on a poor translation of Jesus's words in Matthew 25:32. A good, modern translation of this verse is:

> *All the nations will be gathered before him, and he will separate the people one from another as a shepherd separates the sheep from the goats* (Matthew 25:32 NIV).

Other Bibles translate it in a similar way:

> *Before him will be gathered all the nations, and he will separate people one from another as a shepherd separates the sheep from the goats* (Matthew 25:32 ESV).

And:

> *All the nations will be gathered before him, and he will separate people one from another as a shepherd separates the sheep from the goats* (Matthew 25:32 NRSV).

Similarly:

> *Then all the nations will be arranged before him and he will sort the people out, much as a shepherd sorts out sheep and goats, putting sheep to his right and goats to his left* (Matthew 25:32-33 The Message).

WHY HAVE I BEEN TAUGHT OTHERWISE?

Unfortunately, some of the popular, older Bible translations that you may be familiar with, such as the New American Standard Bible (NASB) and the New King James (NKJV) have a slightly different version of this verse:

> *All the nations will be gathered before Him, and He will separate them one from another, as a shepherd divides his sheep from the goats* (Matthew 25:32 NKJV).

You can see where the common misconception has crept in from these old translations, namely that it is the *nations*, not the people, that will be separated one from another. The NIV Study Bible gives a somewhat technical explanation of how the translators have come about the best way to interpret the original Greek manuscripts:

> All the nations. Both Jews and Gentiles. nations. Greek ethne (neuter plural) sounds at first as if ethnic or people groups will be judged as a whole. But Jesus will actually "separate

the people" (Greek *autous,* "them" [masculine plural] "one from another," referring to the personal judgment of each individual. Palestinian sheep and goats often looked similar from a distance and often grazed together. But they needed to be separated at night because the goats required a warmer place to rest. right...left. The right hand or side of an individual was considered the more honourable; the left, more disgraceful. **(NIV Study Bible – Zondervan)**

In other words, because of the Greek grammar, we can see that the "them" who are being separated are the people, not the nations.

JESUS IS REFERENCING OLD TESTAMENT PROPHETS

All that Jesus was prophesying in this passage would have felt completely familiar to the Jews to whom He was speaking to. Remember that Jesus came first as Messiah to Israel and in these Matthew 24 and 25 parables He was prophesying and warning Israel. The crisis was first theirs, and

He was spelling out the choice that they faced in the starkest of terms. Jesus is putting Israel in the "valley of decision" (see Joel 3).

The Jewish people would have been thoroughly conversant with the Old Testament prophets, such as Ezekiel who often used the language of sheep and shepherds:

> *As a shepherd looks after his scattered flock when he is with them, so will I look after my sheep. I will rescue them from all the places where they were scattered on a day of clouds and darkness. I will bring them out from the nations and gather them from the countries, and I will bring them into their own land. I will pasture them on the mountains of Israel, in the ravines and in all the settlements in the land* (Ezekiel 34:12-13 NIV).

"All the places" and *"from the nations"* and *"from the countries."* Of course, Ezekiel is prophesying first to the scattered exiles of his day (Israel in Babylon) but here we also see a foretelling of the great future gathering of the Gentiles from

across the nations. This incredible chapter concludes with the wonderful verses:

> *Then they will know that I, the Lord their God, am with them and that they, the Israelites, are my people, declares the Sovereign Lord. You are my sheep, the sheep of my pasture, and I am your God, declares the Sovereign Lord* (Ezekiel 34:30-31 NIV).

Who are these Israelites that the prophet is speaking of? You and me! We are His sheep. He has rescued us out from the Gentile, unbelieving nations.

> *I will make a covenant of peace with them...* (Ezekiel 34:25 NIV).

It's the New Covenant! (See Jeremiah 31:31-34, Philippians 4:7).

Now that we have given thanks to God and enjoyed that truth for a moment, we need to go back to why we're looking at this. Did you see the distinction in verse 17? Let's look at it in the English Standard Version:

As for you, my flock, thus says the Lord God: Behold, I judge between sheep and sheep, between rams and male goats (**Ezekiel 34:17**).

And also, "See, I myself will judge between the fat sheep and the lean sheep (Ezekiel 34:20 NIV).

God is telling the Israelites, "I judge between sheep and sheep." This is so important for us to realize. God distinguishes between sheep. Being an Israelite does not guarantee membership in the remnant. You might be sheep in the flock but there's never been a birthright claim to salvation. It's always been about faithful, believing, loyalty to God, ever since Abraham.

And this brings us right back to the prophecy of Jesus, which mirrors the words of Ezekiel:

All the nations [Jews and Gentiles] *will be gathered before him, and he will separate the people one from another as a shepherd separates the sheep from the goats* (**Matthew 25:32 NIV**).

This is why we can be confident that Jesus is not talking about "sheep nations" and "goat nations"—which should be a relief for those of us who live in very rebellious countries!

There's so much more that we can find in Eze-kiel 34—more references to Jesus, to Pentecost, and to Revelation—why don't you make a note to study it later?

ABOUT THE AUTHOR

Emma Stark is an Irish prophet, author, and broadcaster, known around the world for her authority, authenticity, and Celtic boldness. A fifth-generation Bible teacher, Emma graduated with a degree in politics and sociology, before embarking on a successful business career.

In 2009, she founded an international prophetic movement, the Global Prophetic Alliance, which she leads with her husband. From its base in Scotland, Emma's team equips hundreds of thousands around the world to hear from God, receive freedom, and be equipped as prophetic warriors.

YOUR *Prophetic* COMMUNITY

Sign up for a **FREE** subscription to the Destiny Image digital magazine and get awesome content delivered directly to your inbox!

destinyimage.com/signup

Sign up for Cutting-Edge Messages that Supernaturally Empower You

- Gain valuable insights and guidance based on biblical principles
- Deepen your faith and understanding of God's plan for your life
- Receive regular updates and prophetic messages
- Connect with a community of believers who share your values and beliefs

Experience Fresh Video Content that Reveals Your Prophetic Inheritance

- Receive prophetic messages and insights
- Connect with a powerful tool for spiritual growth and development
- Stay connected and inspired on your faith journey

Listen to Powerful Podcasts that Propel You into God's Presence Every Day

- Deepen your understanding of God's prophetic assignment
- Experience God's revival power throughout your day
- Learn how to grow spiritually in your walk with God

In the Right Hands, This Book Will Change Lives!

Most of the people who need this message will not be looking for this book. To change their lives, you need to **put a copy of this book in their hands.**

Our ministry is constantly seeking methods to find the people who need this anointed message to change their lives. **Will you help us reach these people?**

Extend this ministry by sowing three, five, ten, or *even more* books today and change people's lives for the better! Your generosity will be part of catalyzing the Great Awakening that many have been prophesying and praying for.